Table of Contents

The Dynamics of Morality

A Cliodynamic Perspective on Society and Culture

by

Dr. ant

No part of this book may be reproduced in any form or by any electronic or mechanical means including information storage and retrieval systems, without permission in writing from the author. The only exception is by a reviewer, who may quote short excerpts in a review.

Although the author and publisher have made every effort to ensure that the information in this book was correct at press time, the author and publisher do not assume and hereby disclaim any liability to any party for any loss, damage, or disruption caused by errors or omissions, whether such errors or omissions result from negligence, accident, or any other cause.

This publication is designed to provide accurate and authoritative information with regard to the subject matter covered. It is sold with the understanding that the publisher is not engaged in rendering professional services. If legal advice or other expert assistance is required, the services of a competent professional should be sought.

The fact that an organization or website is referred to in this work as a citation and/or a potential source of further information does not mean that the author or the publisher endorses the information the organization or website may provide or recommendations it may make.

Please remember that Internet websites listed in this work may have changed or disappeared between when this work was written and when it is read.

The Dynamics of Morality: A Cliodynamic Perspective on Society and Culture

Contents

Introduction: The Foundations of Cliodynamics and Its Purpose

The study of human societies and their trajectories through history is a pursuit as ancient as the societies themselves. Cliodynamics, an interdisciplinary area of research that merges historical data with mathematical models, stands as a formidable architecture enabling a scientific analysis of cultural and social evolution. This interdisciplinary field is fundamentally rooted in the recognition that stability and change within societies follow discernible patterns. The purpose of this scholarly endeavor is not merely to observe but to understand the dynamics that have shaped human civilization from its inception to the present—and potentially to forecast future developments.

At the threshold of this ambitious study, we acknowledge the rich tapestry of human culture as not only a product of economic, political, and social forces but also as deeply entrenched in the spiritual and moral fabric that Judeo-Christian values have provided. Cliodynamics serves as a robust framework to illuminate the significance of these values and mores in the cultivation and sustenance of societal coherence.

The traditional family, long revered as the nucleus of social order, demands a central focus in our analysis. Through the lens of cliodynamics, we aim to advocate for its place as the cornerstone of culture and society, steadfast against the erosive currents of modernity. The esteem for such fundamental institutions stems from their proven durability and in their nurturing of the civic virtues that ensure the continuity of a well-ordered society.

Our investigation will scrutinize the disruptive forces that threaten to destabilize the social equilibrium. Foremost among these are practices that undermine life's sanctity, such as abortion and euthanasia. Contraception, too, as a facilitator of a hedonistic lifestyle, carries implications that reverberate through the fabric of society. These subjects are approached not with prejudgment but with the objective analytical rigor that befits true scientific inquiry.

In the same vein, the growing acceptance of homosexuality and transgenderism presents new challenges to traditional moral frameworks. While these phenomena are not new to the human record, their current prominence invites a comprehensive cliodynamic examination of their effects on the historical, cultural, and moral landscape.

Cultural shifts and societal transformations bring with them an erosion of previously held moral standards. Through methodical statistical analysis, we shall trace the patterns of these changes and their effects on community cohesion, law, education, and overall welfare. Moral relativism, the intellectual offspring of such transformations, will also be subjected to a scrutinous cliodynamic evaluation.

Law and policy, undeniably influential in shaping societal values, warrant a thorough dissection under the cliodynamic spotlight to understand how legislative actions both reflect and dictate moral outcomes. Furthermore, the enforcement of morality through policing and the community's role in maintaining standards is of prime interest in our discourse on societal evolution.

Education emerges as another salient influence on culture and morality. The historical and future directions of curriculum development and their impact on molding the moral fiber of the young are crucial components of our analysis. Similarly, the role of activism in shaping public opinion through both movements and social change is acknowledged as a potent force requiring careful examination.

As we embark on this journey through the societal landscape, we must also consider the political arena as a critical battleground for moral ideologies. Politicians, with their power to sway public opinion and enact policies, occupy a decisive role in cultural dynamics. Their actions and inactions have ripples that extend far beyond their immediate effect.

The media, through its capacity to propagate information and influence perspectives on morality, enters our purview. The discrete and not-so-discrete messaging embedded within news, entertainment, and even what is derided as propaganda must be addressed for its potential to shape—and misshape—public perception.

No analysis of society would be complete without envisioning the moral implications of economic systems. Our scrutiny extends from the ethos behind capitalism and socialism to the interconnection between wealth and morality. These discussions are enriched by the consideration of how moral considerations can and do permeate economic policies and practices.

Advancements in science and technology inevitably introduce new ethical dilemmas. This new frontier poses profound questions about the interplay between moral values and technological progression. As we explore these advancements and their social impacts, we aim to provide a moral compass to guide us through these uncharted waters.

In an increasingly globalized world, cultural homogenization poses its own set of challenges to the preservation of distinct cultural identities and the integrity of longstanding traditions. Our cliodynamic approach seeks to understand these challenges while also seeking to preserve the diversity of human experience.

Facing the rise of secularism and the corresponding decline of religious influence, we are compelled to measure its impact statistically and understand its trajectory. The future of religion in public life, and specifically the place of Judeo-Christian morals and teachings, is a critical question for our time and one that requires serious and thoughtful reflection.

As we architect our journey through the vast edifice of human cultural evolution, we shall finally turn our gaze to the strategies aimed at restoring the moral foundations of society. Herein lies the potential for reinvigorating the values that have long underpinned the prosperity and harmony of past civilizations. It is within our grasp to help choreograph a future that reveres tradition even as it embraces progress.

Understanding Cliodynamics

Cliodynamics is an intricate mosaic of history, mathematics, and social science that offers a prism through which the past informs the future. At its core, this discipline endeavors to understand the deep tectonic forces that shape societies over long stretches of time. But what makes cliodynamics particularly fascinating is its unwavering commitment to empirical rigor, leveraging advanced statistical tools and computational simulations to dissect the complex web of human interactions and societal trends.

The genesis of cliodynamics is a testament to humanity's perennial quest to discern patterns in the chaos of history. Just as astrophysicists explore the cosmos for underlying principles, cliodynamicists sift through historical data to identify recurring themes and trends. It's a science as robust as it is ambitious, seeking not only to map the past but also to project future societal trajectories.

One cannot overstate the influence of evolutionary theory in the realm of cliodynamics. It posits that societies evolve, much like organisms, through processes of variation, selection, and inheritance. This perspective allows us to discern the forces that have historically guided human societies towards complexity and adaptation. It's a perspective that casts historical phenomena, whether wars, revolutions, or social reforms, as elements in a broader evolutionary narrative.

Yet, cliodynamics is more than abstract theorization; it's deeply rooted in empirical analysis. Through the meticulous compilation of historical databases, cliodynamicists employ statistical models and simulations to test theories about social dynamics. This scientific method sets cliodynamics apart, offering a tangible framework to evaluate hypotheses about societal evolution and decline.

Among the tools in the cliodynamic arsenal, complexity science emerges as a particularly potent ally. By viewing societies as complex systems, cliodynamicists can explore how simple rules at the individual level give rise to intricate patterns at the societal scale. This approach sheds light on how minor changes can precipitate significant societal shifts, thus offering profound insights into the dynamics of social revolutions, the rise and fall of empires, and the evolution of economic systems.

In marrying the abstract elegance of mathematical models with the gritty realism of historical data, cliodynamics provides a rigorous scientific foundation for examining the evolution of societies. It challenges the notion that history is merely a series of unconnected events, propelling the idea that beneath the chaos, there are underlying patterns that, once understood, can offer predictions about the future.

The implications of this approach are expansive, touching upon various spheres of human endeavor. For policymakers, an understanding of cliodynamics can inform more resilient societal structures. For educators, it underscores the importance of historically informed curricula that recognize the dynamic nature of social systems. For community activists, it offers insights into the mechanisms of social change, pointing towards strategies that can harness the inherent dynamics of societies for progressive ends.

Yet, for all its scientific rigor, cliodynamics does not lose sight of the moral dimensions of history. In analyzing the rise and fall of societies, it implicitly raises questions about the values that sustain them. This perspective is crucial in a time when traditional moral and ethical frameworks are under unprecedented scrutiny. By examining historical trends through the lens of cliodynamics, we gain insights into the consequences of societal choices and the importance of preserving those values that have historically contributed to the flourishing of civilizations.

At the intersection of history, mathematics, and social science, cliodynamics stands as a beacon of interdisciplinary inquiry. As we delve deeper into the understanding of our past, it holds the promise of not only illuminating the road traveled but also guiding us towards a future where societal evolution is both understood and, to some extent, predictable. In a world brimming with uncertainties, the clarity offered by cliodynamics is both refreshing and essential.

In conclusion, cliodynamics is not merely an academic pursuit; it's a lens through which we can critically examine the tapestry of human history. Its insights are invaluable for anyone concerned with the dynamics of social change and the preservation of those moral and ethical foundations that have served as the bedrock of civilizations. As we stand on the precipice of profound societal transformations, understanding the forces that have shaped human societies becomes not just an intellectual exercise but a moral imperative.

The Rise of a New Science

In the quest to understand the fabric that weaves together human society and its history, a revolutionary field emerges, bridging the past with predictive possibilities: cliodynamics. This nascent science, predicated on the belief that historical events can be quantitatively analyzed and future patterns predicted, offers a beacon of insight into the cyclical nature of civilization. Its rise marks a confluence of historical scholarship, mathematical rigor, and computational prowess, enabling scholars to unravel the complex interplay of factors that have sculpted human societies across millennia.

At the heart of cliodynamics is the principle that societal dynamics, much like the laws of physics, are governed by underlying patterns that can be discerned through rigorous analysis. This science aspires to do for history what Newton did for the physical world, introducing a framework where the chaos of human events is seen through the lens of order and predictability. It draws upon a vast array of disciplines, from sociology and economics to the hard sciences, employing advanced statistical models and computational simulations to forecast societal trends. This synthesis of knowledge not only challenges traditional historical narratives but also provides a foundation for a more rational understanding of human endeavors.

The relevance of cliodynamics to a diverse audience, including Roman Catholics, sociologists, and policy-makers, cannot be understated. It offers a lens through which the implications of abandoning Judeo-Christian values and the erosion of traditional family structures can be examined, not merely as moral failings but as phenomena with profound societal impacts. By quantitatively analyzing historical shifts in moral standards, cliodynamics provides empirical evidence to support arguments in favor of the traditional family as the cornerstone of stable societies and exposes the damaging consequences of modern societal trends such as abortion, transgenderism, and the decline of religious influence.

In its rigorous pursuit of understanding, cliodynamics transcends mere academic curiosity. It stands as a testament to the power of interdisciplinary inquiry, bolstering the case for traditional values not with rhetoric but with data. As societies grapple with rapid changes and moral relativism, the insights offered by this new science serve as a critical tool for those advocating for a return to the principles that have historically underpinned civilization's greatest advances. Through its empirical analyses, cliodynamics empowers advocates of Judeo-Christian ethics, offering them a robust platform to argue against the currents of societal decay.

However, the climb towards widespread acceptance and integration of cliodynamics into public discourse is steep. As it challenges entrenched narratives and introduces complexity to seemingly straightforward historical interpretations, its proponents must navigate skepticism and inertia. Yet, the potential it holds for enlightening and informing debates on moral and societal issues makes it an indispensible ally in the quest to reinvigorate the moral foundations of society. Through the lens of cliodynamics, we acquire not just a predictive tool, but a mirror reflecting the consequential outcomes of our moral choices, beckoning us towards a path of restoration and coherence.

Evolutionary Theory and Historical Patterns Evolutionary theory, deeply rooted in the biological sciences, has over the decades migrated into the realm of social science, offering a fertile framework for understanding the complex development of societies over time. Within this context, the intersection of evolutionary theory and historical patterns presents a compelling avenue for investigating the manifestations and consequences of human behavior on societal structures, particularly through the lens of Judeo-Christian values.

The concept of evolutionary psychology posits that many human behaviors can be understood as adaptations to challenges faced by our ancestors, which have been encoded in our genes through natural selection. This perspective, when applied to historical patterns, suggests that societal structures and norms, including those rooted in Judeo-Christian values, have emerged and persisted because they serve adaptive functions that have historically contributed to the cohesion and survival of communities.

For example, the institution of marriage, central to Judeo-Christian tradition, can be viewed through an evolutionary lens as a mechanism for ensuring cooperative breeding, social stability, and the successful rearing of offspring. This view aligns with sociobiological perspectives that underscore the importance of kinship and reciprocal altruism as drivers of social organization and moral codes.

Additionally, the Judeo-Christian emphasis on virtues such as fidelity, honesty, and charity can be interpreted as evolutionary strategies for reinforcing social bonds and facilitating cooperative behavior, vital components for group survival in a historical context. These values, when institutionalized within religious traditions, have played a significant role in shaping the moral landscape of societies, guiding behavior, and norms across centuries.

From a cliodynamic perspective, the persistence and influence of Judeo-Christian values can be analyzed through statistical and computational models that explore the dynamics of cultural evolution. By examining historical data, researchers can identify patterns in the rise, spread, and sometimes decline of moral and cultural norms, shedding light on the underpinning mechanisms of social cohesion and moral regulation.

One could argue, harnessing evolutionary theory's principles, that societies which embraced Judeo-Christian values exhibited certain adaptive advantages. These may include enhanced group solidarity, more effective regulatory norms, and a deeply rooted sense of community and purpose, all of which contribute to the resilience and longevity of civilizations.

However, the interaction between evolutionary processes and cultural evolution is complex. While biological evolution is slow and driven by genetic changes, cultural evolution is much more dynamic, allowing for rapid shifts in societal norms and values. This dichotomy presents a unique challenge in understanding how deeply ingrained moral and ethical constructs, such as those derived from Judeo-Christian tradition, adapt and transform in the face of swift societal changes.

Moreover, the application of evolutionary theory to the understanding of historical patterns raises questions about determinism and free will. While some behaviors can indeed be traced back to evolutionary adaptations, human societies also demonstrate a notable capacity for reflection, innovation, and moral reasoning beyond mere survival strategies. This capacity suggests that while evolutionary theory can offer valuable insights into the origins and persistence of certain societal structures and norms, it is not the sole determinant of human behavior and cultural evolution.

In considering the path forward, it becomes evident that the lens of evolutionary theory, supplemented by the methods of cliodynamics, offers a powerful framework for examining the development and significance of Judeo-Christian values within societal evolution. By blending the scientific rigor of evolutionary psychology with the rich historical narrative of human societies, researchers can better understand the role of these values in promoting social cohesion, moral development, and the overall flourishing of communities.

Furthermore, the critical examination of evolutionary theory and historical patterns in relation to Judeo-Christian values opens pathways for dialogue about the adaptability and relevance of these values in contemporary society. As societies continue to evolve at an unprecedented pace, fueled by technological advancements and global interconnectedness, understanding the adaptive functions of traditional moral values could provide insights into addressing modern societal challenges.

The interplay between our evolutionary heritage and the historical accumulation of cultural knowledge, particularly that which is encapsulated in religious traditions, underscores the complexity of human social organization. It also highlights the need for a multidisciplinary approach that embraces the insights of evolutionary theory, history, sociology, and theology in dissecting the fabric of human societies.

In conclusion, the exploration of evolutionary theory and historical patterns offers a nuanced understanding of the development and endurance of Judeo-Christian values within the tapestry of human history. Through a careful analysis of these dynamics, society can better appreciate the contributions of these values to human progress and contemplate their role in navigating the challenges of the modern world.

Statistical Tools and Computational Simulations

In the analytical voyage of understanding the dynamics of historical patterns and societal transformations, statistical tools and computational simulations stand as indispensable beacons. At the core of cliodynamics, an emergent discipline that scrutinizes the cyclical nature of history through the lens of mathematical rigor, lies the robust application of these methodologies. Through the judicious deployment of statistical analyses, scholars of cliodynamics unlock fascinating insights that shimmer with clarity amid the vast sea of historical data, shedding light on the undercurrents shaping societal evolution.

Computational simulations, in particular, offer a window into the complexities of social systems. These dynamic models allow researchers to simulate various scenarios, testing how changes in one part of society may ripple through others. Such simulations often draw upon the concepts of complexity science, which appreciates that social systems are more than the sum of their parts. They behave in unpredictable ways and exhibit patterns and structures emergent from the interactions of their individual components. Thus, through the lens of computational models, the intricate dance of societal forces can be appreciated in its full complexity, unveiling the impact of phenomena like moral decay, religious shifts, and the crumbling of traditional family structures on societal cohesion.

What sets cliodynamics apart in its ambition to employ statistical tools and computational methods is not just the pursuit of knowledge for its own sake, but a moral imperative. The statistical elucidation of historical trends serves as a clarion call to societies veering away from Judeo-Christian values, highlighting the perilous consequences of abandoning the moral and familial compass that has historically guided civilizations towards prosperity and stability.

For instance, through the surgical precision of statistical analysis, the disintegration of the traditional family unit and its correlations with increased societal unrest, crime, and moral relativism can be quantitatively demonstrated. These aren't mere numbers and models; they're a reflection of lived human experience, echoing the profound dissonance wrought by modernity's assault on time-honored values.

Moreover, the predictive power embedded within computational simulations offers a glimpse into potential futures, shaping our understanding of the outcomes societies might face should they continue down paths of moral and ethical neglect. It's a tool not just for understanding but for warning and preparation, enabling policymakers, educators, and community leaders to craft strategies rooted in the wisdom of our forebears, aiming to recalibrate our moral compasses.

However, the application of these statistical and computational methodologies is not without its challenges. The complexity of human societies, influenced by a near-infinite matrix of variables, injects a level of uncertainty into even the most sophisticated models. Yet, it is within this space of uncertainty that the intrinsic value of Judeo-Christian morals – emphasizing human dignity, integrity, and the sanctity of the traditional family – shines brightest. These values provide a stable foundation upon which to build our simulations and forecasts, guiding the interpretation of data through the lens of moral certainty.

It's through the statistical validation of the benefits stemming from adherence to Judeo-Christian values that this analytical journey finds its purpose. The narratives woven in numbers and models speak volumes, urging societies to reflect upon the currents directing their course. Indeed, statistical tools and computational simulations in cliodynamics don't just narrate the past; they illuminate the path forward, advocating for a resurgence in moral and ethical consciousness that aligns with the foundational tenets of Judeo-Christian doctrine.

As we venture further into the intricacies of cliodynamics, let us not lose sight of the moral imperatives that guide our inquiry. The statistical and computational frameworks we deploy are more than mere academic exercises; they are the bearers of truth, entrusted with the grave task of charting a course towards moral revival and societal renewal. In the vast expanse of history, let these tools serve not only to illuminate the consequences of our moral choices but to inspire a recommitment to the values that have, time and again, proved indispensable to the flourishing of civilizations.

In conclusion, the marriage of statistical tools and computational simulations with cliodynamics offers a potent framework for understanding the cyclical nature of history and society's evolution. Through this lens, the critical importance of adhering to Judeo-Christian values and the traditional family structure becomes not just a philosophical stance but a scientifically grounded imperative. As we navigate the complexities of society, let us lean on these methodologies to guide our communities back to the moral bedrock upon which lasting prosperity and peace are founded.

The Role of Complexity Science in Understanding Society

Continuing from our exploration of cliodynamics and its significance, we delve into a crucial sub-discipline that enriches our comprehension of historical and social dynamics: complexity science. Complexity science, with its roots in systems thinking and the study of emergent properties, offers a unique lens through which we can analyze societal structures and phenomena.

At its core, complexity science seeks to understand how parts of a system give rise to the collective behaviors of the system, and how the system interacts with its environment. This approach is not linear; it doesn't view societal change as the result of straightforward, cause-and-effect relationships. Instead, it acknowledges the multifaceted interactions and feedback loops that characterize real-world systems. In doing so, complexity science can illuminate the intricate dynamics of social systems, highlighting how small changes can lead to significant societal shifts.

In the context of understanding society, complexity science's perspective is invaluable. Society is not a monolith; it's a complex adaptive system composed of individuals and institutions, all interacting within an ever-changing array of cultural, economic, and environmental factors. These interactions are not merely additive but synergistic, producing emergent phenomena that cannot be predicted by examining the system's components in isolation. Complexity science thus challenges reductionist viewpoints, advocating for a holistic look at the tapestry of societal interactions.

One of the quintessential applications of complexity science in understanding societal dynamics is in studying the evolution and impact of moral values and structures. This analysis is particularly significant in our discussion, as we're arguing for the central role that Judeo-Christian values play in shaping societies. Through the lens of complexity science, we can see how these values, acting as guiding principles for countless individuals, interact with other social factors to produce the unique fabric of a society.

Moreover, complexity science helps us perceive the resilience and adaptability of societal structures like the traditional family. It shows us how these structures, underpinned by Judeo-Christian moral values, have evolved over time to address the needs of society while maintaining their core functions. This understanding is crucial in today's context, where the traditional family is under siege by modern ideologies and practices like transgenderism, homosexuality, and contraception that diverge from these values.

This science also enables us to grasp the non-linear impacts of contemporary social issues like abortion and immorality. We can examine how such practices, when normalized within a society, not only undermine the sanctity of life and moral standards but also trigger broader systemic effects, disrupting the socio-cultural balance and contributing to societal degradation.

Complexity science encourages a proactive approach to societal problems. Recognizing that small interventions can lead to large-scale change empowers community activists, legislators, and individuals alike to take steps towards reinforcing Judeo-Christian values in society. This aligns with our book's goal of advocating for these values as the cornerstone of culture and society.

Moreover, in the arena of policy analysis and legislative action, applying complexity science offers a methodological advantage. It allows for a more nuanced understanding of how policies rooted in Judeo-Christian moral principles can foster societal well-being, acknowledging the interconnectedness of legal, moral, and cultural domains.

Another dimension where complexity science proves indispensable is in education. It suggests that curricula rooted in traditional moral values can profoundly influence the moral compass of future generations, underpining societal cohesion and resilience against moral relativism and secular challenges.

Furthermore, in addressing the multifaceted crises of prostitution and human trafficking, complexity science reveals the interconnectedness of economic, legal, and societal factors. It shows how interventions that reinforce moral values and seek to protect human dignity can disrupt the cycles that fuel these degradations of human rights.

From an analytical standpoint, complexity science also bolsters our understanding of cultural trends, including the decline of traditional structures and the erosion of societal cohesion. Through its frameworks, we can decipher the complex interactions leading to these trends, paving the way for targeted strategies to counteract them.

In sum, complexity science enriches our dialogue on societal understanding by emphasizing the dynamic, interconnected nature of social systems. Its application across various societal issues - from the structure of the traditional family to the legislation of moral principles - demonstrates its invaluable role in shaping strategies that uphold Judeo-Christian values.

As we advocate for these values in the face of modern challenges, complexity science serves as a reminder of the power inherent in the intricate interplay of societal components.

It beckons us to a higher level of engagement with the world, urging a deepened understanding and strategic action to cultivate and preserve the moral and cultural fabric of society.

In this journey toward comprehending and influencing society, the marriage of complexity science with cliodynamics offers a compelling approach. It not only enriches our analytical toolkit but aligns with our philosophical and moral commitments to nurture a world grounded in enduring values.

Thus, as we forge ahead, embracing the insights of complexity science remains not just an academic endeavor but a moral imperative. It guides us to discern wisely, act compassionately, and advocate tirelessly for the principles that sustain the bedrock of civilization.

The Structure of Society and Culture through History

The fabric of society and culture is complex, interwoven with threads of morality, tradition, and values that have historically been anchored by the influence of Judeo-Christian principles. As the ages have waxed and waned, so too has the prominence of these principles within the public square, shaping the edifice upon which Western civilization stands. These ancient values, emphasizing the sanctity of life, the importance of the traditional family, and a moral compass oriented towards the common good, have acted as the bedrock for societal norms and laws, guiding the progress of nations towards enlightenment and prosperity.

However, as scholars and historians have noted, there has been a marked shift away from these traditional structures and values, particularly in the recent centuries. This decline has been paralleled by an increase in societal issues such as the breakdown of the family unit, a rise in immorality as evidenced by escalating rates of abortion, and the erosion of the sense of community and shared responsibility. The consequences of moving away from a foundation centered on Judeo-Christian values have been profound, leading to a cultural milieu characterized by moral relativism and a disconnection from historical mores that have long been the glue holding society together.

Central to the discourse on the structure of society and culture through history is the understanding of how the decline of these traditional values has shaped the modern landscape. It's impossible to ignore the statistical correlations between the weakening of the traditional family structure and the myriad social challenges that contemporary societies face. Studies have indicated a direct association between these phenomena, suggesting that as societies move away from traditional familial and moral structures, they invariably encounter a host of social maladies ranging from increased rates of crime to a decline in mental health and community cohesion.

This downward trajectory is not simply a matter of sociological interest but represents a clarion call to those who value the contribution of Judeo-Christian principles to the health and prosperity of society. It's a call to reexamine the foundations upon which our cultures are built, to critically assess the impacts of abandoning traditional mores, and to envision a path forward that reincorporates these time-honored values into the fabric of our communities. The task ahead lies not only in identifying the symptoms of societal decay but in advocating for and implementing solutions that address the root causes of this malaise.

In this exploration of the structure of society and culture through history, it becomes clear that a society's strength, cohesion, and moral fortitude are deeply influenced by the values it upholds. As history has shown, societies thrive when they embrace and promote a set of universal moral principles, such as those found in Judeo-Christian ethics. The challenge now is to retrieve what has been lost and to rekindle the flame of traditional values in a way that resonates with contemporary societies, ensuring that the legacy of Judeo-Christian principles continues to guide humanity towards a prosperous and ethical future.

The Influence of Judeo-Christian Values

The profound influence of Judeo-Christian values on the structure of society and culture through history can't be overstated. At the heart of these values lies a profound sense of morality, a compass guiding individuals towards a life of virtue, integrity, and compassion. This moral framework has nurtured societies that cherish the sanctity of life, the importance of family, and the necessity of community cohesion.

From the ancient Hebrew texts, societal laws were established that emphasized justice, equity, and protection for the powerless. These laws weren't just a list of dos and don'ts; they were a reflection of a society's commitment to the wellbeing of its members, particularly those who might otherwise be marginalized or oppressed. Fast forward to the teachings of Jesus in the New Testament, which underscored love, selflessness, forgiveness, and the value of each individual. Together, these Judeo-Christian teachings have laid a foundation for social structures that prioritize human dignity and mutual respect.

Historically, the influence of these values can be seen in the development of legal systems that emphasize individual rights and the common good. Consider, for instance, the concept of the sanctity of life, a cornerstone of Judeo-Christian ethics. This principle has profoundly impacted legislation concerning issues like capital punishment, abortion, and end-of-life care, shaping laws that reflect a profound respect for human life at all stages.

Similarly, the traditional family structure, regarded as the bedrock of society in Judeo-Christian thought, has long been recognized for its role in nurturing the next generations, instilling values of love, responsibility, and respect for others. Societies grounded in these values have consistently shown lower rates of crime, higher educational achievement, and greater psychological wellbeing among their youth.

Moreover, the emphasis on community service and charity in Judeo-Christian teachings has fostered a culture of philanthropy and volunteerism. This spirit of generosity has not only supported countless individuals in times of need but has also strengthened the social fabric, creating more resilient and cohesive communities.

However, the contemporary erosion of these values poses a significant threat to the fabric of society. As secular beliefs gain prominence, the foundational principles that have historically supported ethical behavior and communal responsibility are increasingly dismissed as outdated or irrelevant. The abandonment of these values has coincided with rising trends in family breakdown, social isolation, and moral relativism, suggesting a link between societal health and the influence of Judeo-Christian ethics (Bonham, 2023).

Addressing the degradation of moral standards requires a recommitment to the principles that have proven essential for societal wellbeing. By fostering a culture that values truth, promotes the sanctity of life, and encourages self-sacrifice for the good of others, societies can counteract the corrosive effects of moral decline.

The preservation of traditional family structures is also critical in this endeavor. As the primary environment for the transmission of values and the nurturance of individuals, the family plays a crucial role in the propagation of a healthy, vibrant society. Policies and social norms that strengthen familial bonds and support parents in their vital role can have profound implications for societal health and stability.

In addition to nurturing strong families, the revitalization of community engagement and public morality is imperative. Judeo-Christian ethics, with their emphasis on love, charity, and justice, provide a powerful framework for rebuilding community connections and reestablishing a common moral language that transcends cultural and political divides.

Furthermore, educational efforts that integrate Judeo-Christian perspectives on morality and human dignity can equip future generations with the ethical framework necessary to navigate the complexities of modern life while remaining committed to principles of virtue and integrity.

Legislative actions also play a pivotal role in this process. By enacting and enforcing laws that reflect Judeo-Christian values, societies can protect the vulnerable, promote justice, and encourage a culture of respect and understanding. In this regard, the law serves not merely as a boundary for acceptable behavior but as a reflection of a society's collective moral convictions.

In conclusion, the influence of Judeo-Christian values on the structure of society and culture is both profound and indispensable. These values serve as the foundation for systems of justice, family, community, and morality. As societies face the challenges of moral relativism and cultural fragmentation, a reinvigoration of these fundamental principles offers hope for a more cohesive, vibrant, and ethical future.

The Decline of Traditional Structures

In contemplating the shifts within the fibers of society, a pronounced decline in traditional structures becomes apparent, marking a period of profound transformation. This change does not merely signify an evolution; rather, it hints at a profound unraveling of the threads that have long kept the social fabric cohesive and resilient. At the heart of this decline lies the erosion of the traditional family unit, once hailed as the cornerstone of civilization.

The traditional family, built upon the principles of Judeo-Christian values, has historically served as a bulwark against societal fragmentation. These values, deeply ingrained in the moral and ethical frameworks of numerous societies, have fostered environments where mutual respect, responsibility, and a sense of duty flourish. Yet, as we navigate through the 21st century, the underpinnings of this fundamental institution are being questioned and, in some instances, altogether abandoned.

This shift can be partly attributed to the profound cultural, economic, and technological changes that have collectively reshaped the landscape of human interaction and identity. The introduction of contraception, advancing at a pace unforeseen, has facilitated a disconnection between marital relations and procreation, enabling a view of sexuality that is divorced from its procreative purpose. This separation has nuanced implications, driving a wedge not only between the constituent purposes of marriage but also diluting the societal acknowledgment of its sanctity.

Parallel to this, the legalization and increased social acceptance of practices such as abortion have further contributed to a devaluation of life, challenging the very ethos of family and community (Smith, 2003). These developments have not occurred in isolation but have emerged synergistically, weaving a narrative of autonomy that often conflicts with the tenets of responsibility and interconnectedness that traditional families epitomize.

Moreover, the societal endorsement of diverse gender identities and sexual orientations, while championing the banner of inclusivity and individual rights, has spurred contentious debates around the traditional definitions of marriage and family. The rise of same-sex marriages and the broader acceptance of transgenderism present not only novel legal and social complexities but also philosophical and moral quandaries, particularly within communities rooted in Judeo-Christian doctrines (Williams & Williams, 2020).

Technological advancements, particularly the ubiquity of the internet and social media, have further exacerbated this decline.

The virtual arena, with its promise of unlimited connection, has paradoxically fostered a sense of isolation and detachment from community life. The relentless pursuit of individual identities online often undermines the stability and unity that traditional family structures provide, promoting a culture of transient relationships and diluted kinships.

Faced with these challenges, one might ponder the trajectory of societal evolution. The decline of traditional structures is not merely a phase but a profound transformation that warrants a reevaluation of our societal priorities and values. There is a growing need for a dialogue that transcends the polarizing discourse, recognizing the intrinsic value of traditional institutions while adapting to the changing contours of modern society.

This dialogue must begin with an acknowledgment of the inherent worth of the traditional family as a transmitter of values, morals, and culture. By fostering environments where children learn empathy, respect, and the importance of community, traditional families serve as the primary educators in moral and social responsibilities.

Moreover, the resurgence of community-oriented lifestyles, where individuals collectively partake in each other's lives beyond the digital interface, could serve to counteract the atomization proliferated by modern technology. The essence of community life, grounded in shared values and mutual support, echoes the foundational principles of Judeo-Christian ethics.

Legislation and public policies that support the sanctity of life, marriage, and family also play a critical role. By promoting laws that strengthen family bonds and uphold the dignity of life, societies can create a conducive environment for the flourishing of traditional values.

Religious institutions, moreover, have a pivotal role in this revival. By reasserting their relevance in modern discourse, providing moral and spiritual guidance, these institutions can act as beacons of hope and pillars of strength in times of moral ambiguities.

Ultimately, the challenge lies not in resisting change but in navigating it with wisdom, grace, and a steadfast commitment to the principles that have long underpinned human civilization. The decline of traditional structures offers an opportunity for reflection, innovation, and renewal—a chance to redefine legacy in a manner that is both respectful of its origins and responsive to contemporary needs.

As we tread this path, it's imperative to foster dialogues that bridge divides, understanding that the strength of society lies in its diversity as much as in its unity. In embracing the essence of traditional values while being open to evolution, societies can envision a future that respects the past while boldly stepping into the new frontier.

In conclusion, the decline of traditional structures presents not just a challenge but a clarion call to reengage with the foundational pillars of society. Through thoughtful engagement, legislative support, and community revitalization, there is hope for a resurgence of traditional values in a modern context, ensuring that the legacy of our forebears enriches the lives of generations to come.

The Traditional Family: The Cornerstone of Civilization

The traditional family, often envisioned as a unit comprising two parents and their children, has long been heralded as the fundamental building block of civilization. This chapter delves into the historical perspectives on the family and its undeniable impact on culture and society. The traditional family structure, entrenched in Judeo-Christian values, has not only nurtured individuals but also cemented the very foundations of societies across eras and geographies.

The importance of the traditional family is not merely a matter of cultural preference or historical accident. Psychological and sociological research underscores the critical role that family plays in the development of individuals. The stability, love, and guidance offered by a traditional family environment are pivotal in nurturing well-adjusted individuals (Smith, 2003). The dynamics within these family structures have been shown to foster a sense of responsibility, moral values, and a strong work ethic, contributing significantly to the societal fabric.

Moreover, the traditional family has been a cradle for transmitting cultural norms and values from one generation to the next. This intergenerational transmission is crucial for the continuity and development of civilizations. Each family, through its rituals, traditions, and everyday interactions, instills in its members a sense of belonging, identity, and history. This continuity is not just about preserving the past but about enriching the future by providing stable ground upon which innovation and progress can build.

In contrast, the erosion of traditional family structures in recent decades has coincided with a myriad of social challenges. The rise in divorce rates, single-parent families, and other non-traditional family arrangements has been linked to various adverse outcomes for children and society at large (Nelson, 2020). While it is essential to acknowledge and support all family structures in their diversity, the statistical evidence points to the traditional family as providing the most beneficial environment for raising children.

This is not to say that the traditional family is without its challenges or that it is the only viable family structure. However, understanding and appreciating the unique benefits it offers is crucial in addressing some of the societal issues we face today. The stability and cohesiveness of traditional family units often result in stronger communities, lower crime rates, and higher academic achievements among young people.

From a cliodynamic perspective, the traditional family can be viewed as a stabilizing force throughout history. As civilizations have evolved, the family has remained a constant, adapting to and influencing the course of societal development. The resilience and adaptability of the traditional family are testament to its indispensable role in human societies.

It is also worth noting the economic impact of traditional families. Beyond the societal and cultural contributions, traditional families play a significant role in economic development and stability. Through shared resources, mutual support, and collective economic activities, these family units contribute significantly to the economic well-being and resilience of communities.

Confronting the challenges facing traditional families today requires a multifaceted approach. It involves not only reinforcing the inherent values and strengths of these units but also addressing the societal, economic, and political pressures that undermine them. Promoting policies that support families, such as parental leave, affordable childcare, and education, can help to bolster the traditional family structure.

In conclusion, the traditional family remains a cornerstone of civilization, providing countless benefits to both individuals and society. While it faces challenges in the modern world, its fundamental role is as crucial as ever. By reinforcing and supporting traditional family structures, we can address many of the societal challenges we face and build a more stable, prosperous, and cohesive future.

Historical Perspectives on Family

The fabric of civilization is intricately woven with the threads of the family unit. Historically, the traditional family has been the cornerstone upon which societies have risen and flourished. From the early agrarian communities to the complex societies we navigate today, the essence of the family has remained a constant beacon of stability and moral compass. The significance of the family in shaping culture and society cannot be overstated, and its historical evolution offers profound insights into the moral and structural underpinnings of civilizations.

The genesis of the traditional family can be traced back to ancient civilizations, where familial bonds were paramount in ensuring survival and continuity. In these early societies, the family was not merely a social unit but a crucial economic and cultural institution. Each member had roles that were crucial for the collective well-being, reflecting a symbiotic relationship that underscored the moral fibers of society.

Throughout the annals of history, the family has undergone transformations, adapting to the socio-economic and cultural landscapes of their times. Nevertheless, the fundamental principle of the family as a nurturing ground for moral and ethical values has remained a steadfast pillar across epochs. This adaptability, however, has not shielded the family from contemporary challenges that threaten its traditional structure and values.

In the Judeo-Christian context, the family is seen as a divine institution, ordained to mirror the covenantal relationship between humanity and the divine. This perspective imbues the family with a sacred purpose, not only in begetting offspring but in nurturing them within a framework of moral absolutes. The commandments to honor one's parents, to cleave to one's spouse, and to raise children in the fear of the Lord have provided a stable foundation for societies grounded in Judeo-Christian ethics.

However, the past few centuries have witnessed pivotal shifts, challenging the traditional family model. The enlightenment, industrial revolution, and the rise of individualism have each played a role in reshaping perceptions of family. The erosion of communal life and the ascent of personal autonomy have led to a gradual disintegration of the traditional family's cohesion and its moral imperatives.

These shifts have profound implications for society at large. Numerous studies have indicated the pivotal role that family structure plays in the emotional, psychological, and physical well-being of individuals. For instance, children raised in stable, two-parent families have been shown to fare better on average across various measures of success and well-being. This evidentiary support underscores the traditional family's role in cultivating a healthy, well-adjusted citizenry.

The erosion of traditional family values and structures in contemporary society can be linked to a myriad of social ills. Issues such as juvenile delinquency, substance abuse, and a general decline in moral standards can often find their roots in the breakdown of the family unit. The traditional family, with its emphasis on lifelong marriage and parental responsibilities, has a built-in mechanism for socializing children and imparting ethical values, a mechanism that becomes compromised when the family breaks down.

In light of the aforementioned challenges, there is a pressing need to reaffirm the intrinsic value and indispensability of the traditional family. This is not merely a nostalgic yearning for the past but a recognition of the timeless principles that the traditional family embodies. Policy initiatives, community support systems, and educational programs that reinforce the stability and integrity of the family are imperative.

Furthermore, a reinvigoration of Judeo-Christian values within the context of the family can act as a bulwark against the relativism and moral ambiguity pervading modern society. These values offer a solid moral framework that can guide families through the complexities of contemporary life, fostering resilience, compassion, and integrity.

It is imperative, therefore, for society to recognize the historical significance of the traditional family and to work collaboratively toward safeguarding its place within the modern context. Churches, educational institutions, and community organizations all have roles to play in nurturing and supporting families in their essential mission.

In conclusion, the historical perspective on family offers us a lens through which we can discern the foundational importance of the traditional family structure for social stability and moral clarity. As we confront the challenges of the present and future, it behooves us to draw upon the wisdom of the past, recognizing the traditional family as an indispensable cornerstone of civilization. Only by doing so can we hope to nurture societies that are not only prosperous but also virtuous and just.

The Impact of Family Structure on Culture and Society

The traditional family, often lauded as the cornerstone of civilization, is not merely a social unit but the bedrock upon which societies build their cultural edifices. This structure, ideally comprising two parents committed to each other and their offspring, has been the crucible for instilling values, ethics, and morals across generations. Its impact on culture and society is profound and multifaceted, influencing the fabric of communities, the formation of individual identities, and the collective moral compass of civilizations.

Historically, the traditional family has served as the primary educational environment, where children first learn language, social skills, and the rudimentary principles of morality and faith. This primary socialization equips individuals with the tools necessary for navigating the broader societal context, emphasizing the role of the family in transmitting culture and ensuring societal continuity.

In cultures where the traditional family structure is upheld, research has documented higher rates of societal stability, economic prosperity, and lower incidences of crime and delinquency. This correlation can be attributed to the cohesive and supportive environment that the traditional family provides, fostering a sense of security and belonging that is essential for psychological well-being and social development.

Moreover, the traditional family has been instrumental in maintaining social order. By instilling moral values and norms from an early age, families cultivate individuals who are more likely to adhere to societal laws and less likely to engage in behaviors detrimental to social cohesion. This preventive mechanism against social disorder is critical in sustaining peaceful and prosperous communities (Blitsten, 1963).

Yet, the contemporary landscape presents a stark contrast to this historic norm. The traditional family structure is under siege, facing threats from modern societal shifts including increased divorce rates, single parenthood, and the acceptance of alternative family structures. These changes have not come without cost. Statistical analysis reveals a positive correlation between the decline of the traditional family and increased rates of poverty, lower educational attainment, and a rise in mental health disorders among children (Blitsten, 1963).

This degradation of the traditional family unit erodes the very foundations upon which cultures and societies are built. When families fragment, the transmission of cultural values and norms is disrupted, leading to a generational rift in shared moral and ethical standards. This rift not only undermines social cohesion but also jeopardizes the future prosperity and stability of societies.

Furthermore, the erosion of the traditional family structure contributes significantly to the moral relativism pervading modern societies. As the primary source of moral and ethical instruction deteriorates, individuals increasingly seek guidance from less stable and more fragmented sources, such as peer groups or media, often resulting in a pluralistic moral landscape marked by confusion and conflict.

The implications of these changes are far-reaching. Not only do they affect the social fabric, but they also have profound economic consequences. The breakdown of the traditional family structure is linked with increased dependency on social welfare programs and higher rates of incarceration, both of which place a significant financial strain on societal resources.

Despite these challenges, the resilience of the traditional family, as a model, continues to exhibit a remarkable capacity for adaptation and survival. In societies where traditional values are celebrated and upheld, families find innovative ways to navigate the pressures of modern life while preserving their core functions and integrity. This adaptability underscores the inherent strength of the traditional family model, affirming its role as an indispensable pillar of culture and society.

To safeguard the future of civilizations, it is incumbent upon individuals, communities, and policymakers to recognize and reinforce the traditional family structure. Strategic initiatives aimed at supporting families, such as economic incentives for married couples, educational programs that reinforce the importance of stable family units, and social policies that valorize parenting and the sanctity of marriage, are critical.

In conclusion, the traditional family remains an indomitable force shaping the contours of culture and society. Its enduring influence on moral and ethical values, social cohesion, and economic stability cannot be overstated. As societies continue to evolve, the preservation of the traditional family structure will be paramount in maintaining the integrity and prosperity of civilizations across the globe.

The Role of Religion in Shaping Moral Codes

The interplay between religion and moral codes is a fundamental mosaic in the tapestry of human history. The scaffolding upon which societies are constructed owes much to the religious teachings that lay at their core. Throughout the annals of time, Judeo-Christian values, in particular, have served as a compass guiding ethical behaviors and societal norms. This chapter delves into the pivotal role religion plays in sculpting the moral fabric of society.

At the heart of Judeo-Christian tradition is a rich tapestry of moral teachings and principles that have undeniably influenced the development of ethical codes and laws across civilizations. The Ten Commandments, for instance, not only outline a spiritual blueprint but also set forth a societal framework that emphasizes respect, honesty, and integrity. These age-old decrees have transcended religious boundaries, becoming a bedrock for legal systems worldwide.

The erosion of religious influence in contemporary public life raises questions about the shift in moral landscapes. As secularism gains foothold, there's a noticeable recalibration of moral compasses, often leading away from traditional mores toward a more relativistic ethos. This shift is palpable not just in legislative halls but in everyday decisions and behaviors, marking a departure from a time when religious doctrines were the uncontested arbiters of right and wrong.

However, it's imperative to recognize the dynamic capability of religion to foster a collective identity among its adherents, imbuing them with a sense of purpose and direction. This is particularly evident in the way Judeo-Christian teachings advocate for compassion, philanthropy, and justice. Such values don't merely enrich individual lives but stitch together the social fabric, rallying communities around shared principles and goals.

The diminishing role of religion in public discourse has coincided with an uptick in debates surrounding moral relativism. This paradigm posits that what's considered "moral" is fluid and varies across cultures and time periods. The danger here, as some critics argue, is the potential for a drift towards ethical ambiguity, where lines between right and wrong blur. The steadfastness of religious moral codes offers a counterbalance to this, anchoring societal norms in tried-and-tested ethical courses.

It's worth noting that the influence of religion on moral codes is not monolithic. Within the sphere of Judeo-Christian traditions themselves, there exists a multitude of interpretations and practices. Yet, the core ethos of love, respect, and justice permeates through these varying expressions, demonstrating religion's enduring legacy in shaping moral landscapes.

The journey toward understanding the role of religion in moral code formation is akin to navigating a labyrinthine library, where every book is a testament to the profound impact of spiritual beliefs on societal norms. As we sift through historical anecdotes and contemporary analyses, the narrative that emerges is one of religion serving not only as a moral compass but as a builder of communities, a source of consolation, and a beacon of hope.

This chapter, while tracing the contours of religion's influence on moral codes, invites a reflection on the symbiotic relationship between spirituality and societal values. As the world becomes increasingly pluralistic, the dialogue between differing moral philosophies, shaped by diverse religious backgrounds, has the potential to enrich the collective human experience, fostering a deeper understanding and tolerance among varying cultures and traditions.

In conclusion, exploring the role of religion in shaping moral codes uncovers layers of complexity and nuance. The challenge ahead lies in balancing the strengths of religious moral frameworks with the evolving landscape of a globalized, multicultural world. The task is not to resist change but to navigate it with wisdom, drawing from the rich well of religious teachings to inform, guide, and enrich the moral codes that bind societies together.

The interweaving of religious principles with the fabric of societal norms underscores the indelible mark religion has made in crafting the moral edifices upon which civilizations stand. As we venture forth, understanding the dynamics between religion and morality will be crucial in forging pathways that honor the essence of human dignity and the pursuit of a just and equitable society.

Judeo-Christianity's Historical Influence

The influence of Judeo-Christian values on the development of moral codes throughout history is both profound and pervasive. This longstanding tradition has provided the ethical framework for the Western legal systems and continues to underpin many aspects of modern society, despite the growing secularization in many parts of the world. In tracing the timelines of societies and scrutinizing their moral schemas, one cannot ignore the substantial imprint left by Judeo-Christian ethos. The inherent dignity of human life, the significance of the traditional family structure, and the ethical principles governing behavior are among the most consequential contributions stemming from this religious tradition.

Historically, the Ten Commandments have acted as a moral compass for countless individuals and societies, espousing principles that promote justice, personal integrity, and respect for others. Concepts such as the sanctity of human life, the importance of marital fidelity, and the condemnation of theft and falsehood have not only found their home in religious texts but have permeated legal systems and societal norms.

Consider the legal principle of "justice for all," which has its roots deeply embedded in Judeo-Christian doctrine. The Book of Leviticus, for instance, admonishes the practice of partiality in justice, insisting that the poor and the rich be judged with the same standard (Phillips, 1996). This idea has evolved into modern legal principles that emphasize equality before the law, a cornerstone of democratic societies.

The family, as conceptualized in Judeo-Christian ideology, has long been recognized as the foundational unit of society. Historical records attest to the way in which the traditional family structure, centered around a committed marital relationship, has contributed to societal stability and the successful rearing of offspring. The traditional family has been shown to be a crucible for the moral formation of individuals, instilling values such as altruism, responsibility, and societal engagement (Wilcox & Wolfinger, 2008).

Furthermore, in the debate on the sanctity of life, the Judeo-Christian perspective has been a vehement defender of life from conception to natural death. This principle has influenced laws and ethics throughout the centuries, opposing practices that undermine the intrinsic value of human existence. This principle continues to challenge contemporary society to reconsider prevailing attitudes toward issues like abortion and euthanasia.

The ethical teachings derived from Judeo-Christian values have also played a key role in shaping the effort to eradicate social injustices. Movements against slavery, racial discrimination, and the oppression of the weak often found their most passionate advocates among communities driven by their religious convictions. This historical fact underscores the role of Judeo-Christian principles as a catalyst for social reform and the advancement of human rights (Woodberry, 2012).

The tradition's commitment to charity and care for the marginalized is another area where its moral influence is unmistakable. The concept of agape love—selfless, sacrificial, unconditional love—espoused by Judeo-Christianity, has fueled global philanthropic endeavors and support for the destitute. These values laid the groundwork for the modern nonprofit sector and charitable organizations that strive to alleviate suffering and provide for the needy.

In the realms of education and morality, Judeo-Christian ideals have been instrumental in the development of institutions that not only impart knowledge but also focus on character formation. The pursuit of truth and wisdom is deeply entwined in this educational ethos, reflecting the belief in an absolute moral order.

Moreover, the work ethic celebrated in Judeo-Christian teaching has significantly influenced the economic structures of Western societies. The values of diligence, thrift, and integrity in labor have been major contributors to the financial prosperity and social progress witnessed in these nations.

Despite these contributions, there is a discernible shift in contemporary society, where the once pervading influence of Judeo-Christian morality is met with skepticism and the rise of secular ideologies. As moral relativism gains traction, the concept of universal moral absolutes—once grounded in religious tradition—is increasingly challenged (Smith, 2003).

Yet, one must acknowledge the historical durability of Judeo-Christian values and their adaptability to wider sociocultural contexts. They've proven to provide a resilient ethical framework that has withstood the vicissitudes of time. Therein lies the crux of the debate: whether this time-honored moral edifice can persist as a counterbalance to the changing mores of the day or if it will be relegated to the annals of historical footnotes.

This section has endeavored to elucidate the historical influence of Judeo-Christianity as it pertains to the formation and sustenance of moral codes. Its pervasive legacy, while fraught with contemporary contention, cannot be denied its pivotal role in the shaping of moral and ethical standards through history. As the chapters progress, the examination of the current moral landscape will continue with an acute awareness of this foundational influence.

The Diminishing Role of Religion in Public Life

In recent years, we've witnessed a pronounced shift in the landscape of societal values, where the role of religion, particularly the Judeo-Christian tradition, in public life has seen a notable decline. This trend is not an isolated phenomenon but a reflection of broader sociocultural transformations occurring across the globe. The roots of this decline are multifaceted, stemming from advancements in science and technology, the rise of secularism, and a growing emphasis on individualism over communal or collective values.

The diminishing presence of religious principles in the public square has far-reaching implications, impacting not only the moral and ethical framework of society but also its legal and educational institutions. Historical analysis reveals that Judeo-Christian values once served as the cornerstone of moral guidance, providing a foundation for laws, social norms, and community standards. However, as the influence of religion wanes, a vacuum is created, often filled by relativistic and secular ideologies that lack the cohesive and stabilizing force of religious moral codes.

One of the most visible signs of religion's waning influence is the changing landscape of family structures. The traditional family, once the bedrock of society, has undergone significant transformations, with an increase in single-parent households, cohabitation, and divorce rates. These trends, while multifactorial, can in part be attributed to a shift away from religious values that traditionally upheld the sanctity of marriage and family.

Education systems, too, have been affected by the decreasing role of religion. Where religious instruction once played a pivotal role in character development and moral education, secularism has redefined the boundaries of moral and ethical discourse within educational settings. This shift raises questions about the sources of moral authority and the basis of ethical reasoning in the absence of religious moral frameworks.

Legally, the implications of the diminishing role of religion are profound. Legislative bodies and judiciaries increasingly adopt a secular approach to lawmaking and judicial decisions, moving away from principles that were once grounded in religious morality. As a result, laws concerning life, family, and public morality reflect a broad spectrum of beliefs and values, often leading to contentious debates on issues such as abortion, marriage, and freedom of speech and religion.

In the political arena, the decline of religion's influence has led to a polarization between secular and religious viewpoints, with each side advancing fundamentally different visions for society.

This division is not merely ideological but manifests in policy decisions and legislative priorities, further complicating the integration of religious principles into public life (Maryl, 2016).

Public discourse, too, has shifted. Media portrayals of religion often connote intolerance or backwardness, perpetuating stereotypes that undermine religion's role in society. As a result, individuals may feel discouraged from expressing their religious beliefs openly, for fear of social ostracization or professional repercussions.

Despite these challenges, it's important to consider the resilience of religious communities and the enduring relevance of Judeo-Christian values in shaping individual lives and local communities. Across the globe, religious organizations continue to play a crucial role in social services, education, and humanitarian efforts, demonstrating the persistent influence of religious values in addressing societal needs.

The question then arises: What can be done to address the diminishing role of religion in public life? Reinvigorating religious education, fostering interfaith dialogue, and advocating for religious freedoms are potential pathways. By embracing the richness of religious traditions and their contributions to moral and ethical discourse, society can find ways to integrate these values into public life, ensuring a diverse and inclusive public square.

Moreover, individuals and communities have a critical role to play in bridging the gap between religious and secular spheres. Through active engagement in public discourse, advocacy, and community service, believers can demonstrate the relevance and applicability of religious values in addressing contemporary social issues.

In conclusion, the diminishing role of religion in public life presents both challenges and opportunities. As society navigates the complexities of modernity, the need for a moral and ethical compass remains. Judeo-Christian values, with their emphasis on compassion, justice, and human dignity, offer valuable insights for constructing a moral framework that resonates with the contemporary human condition. As we move forward, it is imperative to foster dialogue, understanding, and respect across religious and secular divides, building a society that values the contributions of all its members.

Prostitution and Its Effects on Society

The issue of prostitution, a practice as old as civilization itself, continues to present a complex challenge to societies worldwide. Its impact on society, particularly from a Judeo-Christian value perspective, reflects a degradation of human dignity and moral fabric. Grounded in the principles of cliodynamics, this chapter delves into the historical overview, current statistical trends, and the multifaceted social consequences of prostitution. The objective is to shed light on how this ancient profession undermines the cornerstone of culture and society—the traditional family structure—while also examining its broader implications within the community.

Historically, prostitution has been documented in the earliest civilizations, serving various roles within societies, from religious rituals to a recognized economic sector. Yet, irrespective of its form or legality, prostitution has consistently been at odds with Judeo-Christian morals, which hold the sanctity of marriage and sexual relations within it as central tenets. The persistence of prostitution in modern cities not only challenges these values but also corrodes the essential foundation of societal health and stability: the family unit.

Statistically, the prevalence of prostitution has shown an increasing trend, notably in conjunction with the rise of internet-based platforms that facilitate secretive commercial sexual transactions. This ease of access and perceived anonymity contribute not only to its growth but also to the difficulty in combating its spread. From a sociological perspective, the normalization of sex work as a choice profession undermines the traditional view of sexual intimacy and its reserved place within marriage. Moreover, the commodification of the human body inherently conflicts with the intrinsic worth assigned to each individual within Judeo-Christian teachings.

The degradation of human dignity through prostitution cannot be overstated. Participants, primarily women, endure profound psychological and physical consequences (Miller & Schwartz, 2013). The act of selling one's body is often not one of free will but driven by circumstances such as poverty, addiction, or coercion. This reality starkly contrasts with the Judeo-Christian ideal of freedom and dignity, further highlighting the moral abyss between the two.

The effects of prostitution ripple through society, contributing to a breakdown of community values and standards. Neighbourhoods known for prostitution face increased crime rates, decreased property values, and a general sense of decay. Children raised in these environments are exposed to harmful activities and lifestyles from a young age, distorting their perceptions of normalcy and morality.

Moreover, prostitution is intrinsically linked with human trafficking, a severe violation of human rights and an affront to Judeo-Christian ethics. Victims, often young women and children, are stripped of their autonomy and subjected to unimaginable abuses. This modern-day form of slavery starkly contrasts with the principles of freedom and respect for human life that are central to Judeo-Christian values (Miller & Schwartz, 2013).

To combat the detrimental effects of prostitution on society, it is imperative to reinforce the traditional family structure and restore the moral compass provided by Judeo-Christian teachings. This includes comprehensive efforts to educate, provide alternative employment opportunities, and rehabilitate those affected. Additionally, legislative measures to curb demand and penalize traffickers are crucial.

In summary, prostitution represents a profound challenge to the moral and social order predicated on Judeo-Christian values. Its impact on individuals, families, and communities necessitates a multifaceted and morally grounded approach to address and mitigate its effects. By reaffirming the primacy of the traditional family and the inherent dignity of each individual, society can confront and overcome the scourge of prostitution and its many societal ramifications.

In the next chapters, we will further explore how contemporary issues like human trafficking and the breakdown of communities interconnect with prostitution, emphasizing the urgent need for a moral and societal response.

Historical Overview and Statistical Trends

The evolution of prostitution and its profound impact on society cannot be understood without examining its historical depth and the statistical trends that paint a vivid picture of its social implications. The proliferation of this age-old profession has navigated through centuries, adapting and morphing within the socio-cultural fabrics of civilizations, yet maintaining a constant burden on the moral and ethical scaffolds that uphold society.

Historically, prostitution has been recorded as early as the 6th century B.C. in ancient civilizations, where it often intertwined with religious and economic activities. These early instances underscore a troubling entanglement between the commodification of the human body and societal norms. Yet, it's the persistence and adaptability of prostitution through eras—surviving reformations, revolutions, and legal transformations—that beckon a closer examination.

Statistical trends in recent decades shed light on the escalation of this issue. According to studies, the global sex industry generates an estimated $186 billion annually (Sorensen, 2019). This staggering figure is symptomatic of a deeper societal malaise, reflecting not only on the proliferation of the industry but also on the increasing commodification of human relationships.

In the United States, the advent of the internet and mobile technology has drastically altered the landscape of prostitution, making it more hidden yet pervasive. Online platforms have become havens for solicitation, complicating law enforcement efforts and statistical measurement. Despite this, estimates suggest that up to 10% of men in the country have engaged in transactions with prostitutes. indicative of a societal drift from traditional moral values.

The impacts of prostitution extend beyond mere statistics; they erode the very fabric of societal norms and values. The degradation of human dignity, evident in the transactional nature of prostitution, contradicts the fundamental Judeo-Christian ethos that champions the sanctity of the human body and the purity of sexual relations within the confines of marriage.

Furthermore, the intertwining of prostitution with human trafficking presents a grim picture of exploitation and abuse. The United Nations estimates that a significant proportion of trafficked individuals end up in the commercial sex trade, subject to coercion and violence (United Nations, 2019). This alarming trend not only perpetuates the cycle of abuse but also undermines global efforts to uphold human rights and dignity.

Prostitution's effect on the traditional family structure is another area of concern. The breakdown of marital fidelity, fueled by the accessibility and anonymity of paid sexual services, contributes to the destabilization of the family unit. This erosion of the traditional family affects the societal fabric at its core, leading to a cascade of social issues including child neglect, increased divorce rates, and psychological distress among family members.

Statistical analysis further reveals the public health crisis intertwined with prostitution. The prevalence of sexually transmitted infections (STIs) among prostitutes and their clients is alarmingly high, posing a significant public health challenge. This aspect not only affects individuals engaged in or directly impacted by prostitution but also places a substantial burden on healthcare systems worldwide.

Efforts to combat prostitution through legislation have seen varying degrees of success. Countries adopting the Nordic model, which criminalizes buying sex but not selling it, have reported a reduction in demand and a subsequent decrease in the prevalence of prostitution (Andersson & Gardell, 2019). This approach, focusing on the demand side of prostitution, aligns with efforts to uphold societal moral standards by targeting the root cause of the problem.

However, the path forward demands more than legislation alone. It requires a societal reawakening to the values that esteem human dignity above the commodification of the body. Education and community initiatives play a crucial role in this endeavor, offering pathways for individuals trapped in the cycle of prostitution to find alternatives and rebuild their lives on the foundation of respect and dignity.

The role of religious institutions in this societal challenge cannot be understated. By reaffirming the foundational Judeo-Christian values that advocate for the sanctity of the human body and the sacredness of sexual relations within marriage, religious leaders and communities can provide a moral compass for society. Through outreach, support, and education, they can address the root causes of prostitution, including poverty, inequality, and lack of opportunity, thus fostering environments where individuals are valued for their inherent worth.

In conclusion, the historical overview and the prevailing statistical trends surrounding prostitution reveal a multifaceted challenge that extends beyond the act itself, permeating the social, economic, and moral realms of society. It's a challenge that calls for a unified response, championing the restoration of human dignity and the reinvigoration of traditional family structures as cornerstones of societal health. As we navigate the complexities of this issue, it's imperative to remember that every individual involved is worthy of respect, dignity, and the opportunity for redemption.

It is within the confluence of law, societal action, and moral conviction that the path to addressing the scourge of prostitution lies. By weaving the threads of education, legal reform, and moral rejuvenation into the fabric of society, there is hope for reversing these trends and reinstating the values that uphold the dignity of every human being.

The Degradation of Human Dignity

In examining the effects of prostitution on society, it becomes crucial to delve into the profound ways in which it undermines human dignity. This section will explore the nexus between prostitution and the devaluation of human worth from various angles, demonstrating its corrosive impact on individuals and the broader social fabric.

At its core, prostitution treats individuals not as beings with intrinsic worth but as commodities to be bought and sold. This transactional nature of human interaction erodes the foundational moral principles that uphold the dignity of the person. It elevates the pursuit of pleasure and profit above respect for human life, leading to a society where people are valued not for who they are but for what they can provide.

The commodification of human beings has far-reaching consequences that extend beyond the individuals directly involved. Families, as the basic unit of society, suffer profoundly. The introduction of commercialized sex within a community distorts relational dynamics, fostering environments where exploitation and objectification thrive. Such conditions directly contradict the values that stabilize and enrich family life, eroding the cornerstone of civilization that we have strived so hard to build and maintain.

Furthermore, the normalization of prostitution perpetuates a cycle of poverty and degradation. Individuals, often driven by desperation, enter into prostitution, only to find themselves trapped in a cycle that strips them of their dignity and autonomy. This cycle not only harms the individuals involved but also perpetuates societal inequalities, as the most vulnerable members of society are exploited and dehumanized.

The psychological impact on those involved in prostitution cannot be overstated. The reduction of human beings to objects of gratification inflicts profound emotional and mental trauma. Studies have shown that individuals involved in prostitution experience higher rates of depression, anxiety, and post-traumatic stress disorder (PTSD) (Farley, 2003). The psychological scars left by such experiences undermine the inherent dignity of the individual, casting long shadows over their lives.

In addition to the personal toll, the societal acceptance of prostitution undermines the collective moral fabric. It sends a message that the exploitation and objectification of others is permissible so long as it serves individual desires or economic ends. Such a message is antithetical to the principles of justice, equality, and respect that form the bedrock of moral societies.

Moreover, the legal system's approach to prostitution often accentuates the degradation of human dignity. While there is a growing movement towards decriminalizing the sex workers themselves, the focus remains largely punitive rather than rehabilitative or preventative. This legal stance fails to address the underlying issues that lead individuals into prostitution and does nothing to restore their dignity or offer pathways to a better life.

The portrayal of prostitution in media and popular culture further complicates the issue. Frequently glamorized or trivialized, these portrayals distort the harsh realities faced by those involved. Such misrepresentations not only desensitize society to the suffering and degradation inflicted by prostitution but also hinder efforts to address the root causes and find meaningful solutions.

Efforts to combat the degradation of human dignity must, therefore, be multifaceted. They must address not only the economic and social factors that drive individuals into prostitution but also the cultural and legal frameworks that enable it. Education plays a crucial role in this endeavor, fostering a societal understanding that every individual possesses inherent worth that transcends economic utility or physical desirability.

Moreover, the reinvigoration of moral and ethical teachings that emphasize the sanctity of human life and the dignity of every individual is paramount. These teachings offer a counter-narrative to the commodification of human beings, advocating for a society where individuals are valued for their inherent worth.

Community-based interventions can also play a critical role in addressing the root causes of prostitution. By providing support and resources to those at risk, communities can offer pathways to economic stability and personal empowerment that do not involve degradation or exploitation.

Ultimately, addressing the degradation of human dignity requires a collective commitment to upholding the value of every person. It demands a societal rejection of frameworks that commodify human beings and a concerted effort to foster environments where dignity, respect, and compassion prevail.

In conclusion, the degradation of human dignity through prostitution is a complex issue that touches on moral, social, and economic dimensions of society. It challenges us to reexamine our values and the structures within which we operate, urging a return to principles that affirm the worth and dignity of every individual. Only through such a comprehensive and compassionate approach can we hope to address the profound harms inflicted by prostitution on individuals and society as a whole.

The Economics of Human Trafficking

Human trafficking represents one of the gravest moral failings of our time. It's a phenomenon that starkly contrasts with the fundamental tenets of Judeo-Christian values, challenging the very fabric that holds communities together. At its core, human trafficking denies the inherent dignity and value bestowed upon every individual, reducing human lives to mere commodities for profit. This chapter delves into the economic underpinnings of human trafficking, shedding light on how economic incentives perpetuate this global crisis and offering insights into the breakdown of communities that facilitates its spread.

The role of demand in human trafficking cannot be overstated. It's an economic principle of supply and demand that, unfortunately, applies to this illegal trade as well. Where there is demand, there is always someone willing to supply, even if it means exploiting other human beings. This demand is fueled by the darker sides of human desire, ranging from cheap labor to the sex trade. The profitability of human trafficking, with its low overhead costs and high revenue potential, makes it an attractive venture for criminals.

Economics teaches us that the market responds to incentives. Sadly, the market for human trafficking is no exception. The incentives for traffickers are overwhelmingly compelling: high profits and perceived low risks of capture and prosecution. Additionally, the global nature of today's economies, characterized by vast disparities in wealth and opportunities, creates fertile ground for traffickers to exploit vulnerable populations.

One of the key economic factors contributing to human trafficking is poverty. Poverty not only makes individuals more vulnerable to deception and coercion but also stymies the ability of communities to protect their members. Desperation forces people to leave their homes, seeking better opportunities elsewhere, often leading them directly into the hands of traffickers who promise jobs, stability, and a brighter future, none of which they intend to provide.

The breakdown of communities is both a cause and a consequence of human trafficking. As traditional structures that once offered support and protection erode under the weight of economic hardship, migration, and the infiltration of illicit activities, communities become less cohesive. This disintegration further facilitates trafficking by stripping away the social safety nets that could have prevented it (Sorensen, 2019).

From a sociological perspective, the fragmentation of communities has been linked to broader trends in society, including the decline in traditional family structures and the decreasing influence of religious institutions. These trends not only weaken community bonds but also erode the moral compass that guides individuals, making it easier for traffickers to operate with impunity.

Understanding the economics of human trafficking also means confronting the uncomfortable reality that consumer behavior indirectly fuels this trade. The demand for cheap goods and services incentivizes businesses to cut costs, sometimes by turning a blind eye to the exploitation in their supply chains. This makes consumers complicit in perpetuating the cycle of trafficking, often unknowingly.

Addressing the economic underpinnings of human trafficking requires a multi-faceted approach. Strengthening communities and restoring traditional structures that provide support and guidance can help shield vulnerable populations from traffickers. Moreover, raising awareness about the true cost of cheap goods and services can alter consumer behavior and reduce demand for products linked to human trafficking.

Legislation and enforcement play critical roles in disrupting the economic incentives for human trafficking. By increasing the risks associated with trafficking, through tougher penalties and more rigorous enforcement, the economic equation begins to shift. Traffickers face higher costs, both in terms of potential legal ramifications and the need to evade detection, which can diminish the attractiveness of this illicit trade.

Ultimately, the battle against human trafficking is not just economic or legal; it's fundamentally moral. By reaffirming our commitment to Judeo-Christian values, emphasizing the sanctity of human life, and fostering a culture that values every person's dignity, we can begin to unravel the economic fabric of human trafficking. It's a call to action, urging us to live out the ideals we profess to believe in and making it clear that exploiting our fellow human beings for profit is unequivocally unacceptable.

Education is another powerful tool in this fight. By informing communities about the dangers of human trafficking and educating them on how to protect themselves and their loved ones, we can build resilience against traffickers. Knowledge empowers individuals, enabling them to make informed decisions and recognize the signs of trafficking, thereby reducing their susceptibility to exploitation.

Religious institutions also have a crucial role to play. By leveraging their moral authority and community networks, these institutions can spread awareness, offer support to victims, and reinforce the moral imperatives against exploitation. Their involvement can inspire action, foster a culture of care, and provide a moral framework that condemns the commodification of human lives.

In conclusion, the economic dynamics of human trafficking present significant challenges, but they also offer clear pathways for intervention. By identifying and targeting the economic incentives at the heart of human trafficking, society can undermine the foundations of this illicit trade. It requires a concerted effort from individuals, communities, businesses, and governments, all guided by a moral compass that refuses to tolerate the exploitation of any human being. Judeo-Christian values, with their emphasis on the innate worth of each person, provide a solid foundation for these efforts. It's a battle that demands our attention, our compassion, and, most importantly, our action.

Strengthening the moral and social fabric of our communities, reaffirming the importance of traditional family structures, and revitalizing the role of religious institutions are not just ideological goals; they are indispensable strategies in the fight against human trafficking. As we move forward, let us remember that the economics of human trafficking are inextricably linked with the moral choices we make every day. By choosing to act, to care, and to protect, we can dismantle the economic structures that support this heinous crime and rebuild a world where freedom and dignity are afforded to all.

The Role of Demand in a Global Crisis

The intricate tapestry of our global society is marred by the blemishes of various crises, amongst which human trafficking stands out for its sheer inhumanity and scale. Essential to understanding this crisis, particularly through the lens of economic dynamics, is the pivotal role of demand. Demand, in its most nefarious form, fuels the smuggling and exploitation of human lives, creating a market where individuals are reduced to commodities in a profoundly disturbing violation of the dignity inherent to the human person.

At the heart of this crisis is a stark, uncomfortable reality: without demand, there would be no supply. This fundamental economic principle takes a dark turn when applied to human trafficking. It unveils the grim truth that there exist forces within our global society that perpetuate and sustain a demand for exploitative labor and sexual services. This demand does not exist in a vacuum; it is the outcome of a complex web of societal failures, including the erosion of traditional moral values and the breakdown of the family unit.

The traditional Judeo-Christian moral framework, which emphasizes the sanctity of human life and the importance of the family, serves as a bulwark against the devaluation of human dignity. However, as secular ideologies gain ground and the influence of religion in public life diminishes, the foundational beliefs that protect and uphold the value of every individual are being eroded. This moral decay creates fertile ground for the justifications and rationalizations that feed into the demand for human trafficking.

Furthermore, the breakdown of communities and the decline of traditional structures contribute to the vulnerability of individuals to trafficking. In societies where the family unit is under siege, and community bonds are weakening, individuals become more susceptible to the false promises of traffickers. The absence of strong, supportive networks leaves many with no choice but to place their trust in the hands of those who would exploit them.

Economic desperation plays a significant role as well. In a world where wealth is idolized, and material success is often placed above moral integrity, the commodification of human beings becomes a more palatable concept. This desperation, coupled with a lack of moral guidance, pushes both the demand and supply sides of human trafficking.

The global nature of this crisis means that addressing demand must also be a global effort. It requires the reevaluation of societal values and a concerted effort to reinforce the integrity of the family unit as the cornerstone of a moral society. Policies that aim to reduce economic desperation and to provide viable alternatives to those at risk of being trafficked are also critical.

Legislation plays a crucial role in curbing demand. Implementing and enforcing stricter laws against all forms of exploitation, alongside international cooperation to dismantle trafficking networks, can reduce the profitability of human trafficking. However, legal measures alone are not sufficient. They must be accompanied by a cultural shift that reestablishes the sanctity of human life and the importance of moral values in guiding our choices and behaviors.

Education is another powerful tool in combating the demand for human trafficking. Awareness campaigns can illuminate the reality of trafficking, dispelling myths and exposing the human suffering behind the statistics. Education can also promote the values of empathy, respect, and dignity, fostering a societal ethos that is fundamentally incompatible with the exploitation of human beings.

Community initiatives that focus on strengthening families and communities could also mitigate the factors that feed into the demand for trafficking. By providing support and resources to vulnerable populations, these initiatives can reduce the allure of traffickers' promises and create a more vigilant and protective societal network.

The role of religion and faith-based organizations in addressing demand should not be underestimated. These entities can offer spiritual guidance, moral education, and practical support to those at risk, while also championing the cause of human dignity in the public sphere. Their involvement can galvanize communities to action, fostering a culture of care and respect that directly counters the commodification of human lives.

Addressing the demand in a global crisis like human trafficking is an immense challenge that requires a multifaceted approach. It involves not only legal and economic strategies but, crucially, a commitment to the values that affirm the worth and dignity of every individual. As society navigates this crisis, it must do so with the recognition that every effort to diminish demand is a step towards reaffirming the sanctity of human life.

In conclusion, the scourge of human trafficking, fueled by demand, is a stark reminder of the consequences of moral decay and societal fragmentation. It is a call to action for individuals, communities, and nations to recommit to the principles of justice, dignity, and respect for life. By addressing the demand head-on, society can weaken the chains of exploitation and take a stand for the inherent value of every person.

The Breakdown of Communities

At the heart of a community's prosperity and moral vigor lies the intertwining fibers of family, faith, and social cohesiveness. It is through these integral constructs that societies have historically thrived, shaping environments conducive to the flourishing of human dignity and liberty. Nevertheless, the dark underbelly of human trafficking unveils a grim narrative, one that paints a stark picture of the breakdown of these communal bastions. This breakdown is not merely a symptom but a catalyst for further societal decay, perpetuating a cycle of vulnerability and exploitation.

The intricate economics of human trafficking reveal a perverse exploitation of humanity's brokenness. Communities fragmented by social, economic, and moral upheavals find themselves in the throes of vulnerability. This susceptibility is not a happenstance but a calculated target of traffickers who prey on the disenfranchised, the marginalized, and those stripped of the protective veil of community and familial bonds. It's a cruel irony that the breaking of these bonds does not just allow trafficking to flourish but ensures its victims are often invisible, hidden within the fractures of community itself.

Broken families, a plague upon the modern age, serve as fertile grounds for traffickers. The traditional family model, once the cornerstone of societal stability and moral instruction, now faces unprecedented assaults, leading to its alarming erosion. This disintegration fosters an environment where the young and vulnerable are easily misled and lured away under the guise of love, opportunity, or sheer desperation, making them ripe for exploitation.

Moreover, the decline in religious adherence and community engagement has torn down the moral guardrails that once offered protection. These institutions, responsible for the moral education and character building of individuals, now find their influence waning. Without these, individuals lack the discernment needed to navigate and resist the snares set by traffickers, illustrating a direct correlation between diminished moral standards and increased trafficking vulnerabilities.

The economics of demand in human trafficking are complex, reflecting a society's moral health or lack thereof. The demand for cheap labor and sexual exploitation, symptomatic of unbridled consumerism and moral decay, drives the trafficking industry. This demand does not exist in a vacuum but is cultivated by communities that have abandoned principles of dignity, self-restraint, and respect for human life.

Compounding this issue is a globalized economy where human lives are commoditized, feeding an insatiable demand for labor and sexual exploitation. This global marketplace, while offering economic opportunities, also opens the floodgates to unprecedented levels of exploitation. It reflects a stark departure from a communal ethos that values every member, showing a preference instead for economic gain at a devastating human cost.

Technological advances, though potential forces for good, have also facilitated the proliferation of trafficking networks, making it easier for perpetrators to operate with anonymity and reach a broader audience. The digital age, while bringing people closer in some respects, has paradoxically contributed to a more profound sense of isolation and disconnection within communities, making individuals more susceptible to exploitation.

Urbanization and the dissolution of rural communities have ushered in unique challenges. The migration to urban centers in search of better opportunities often results in the disintegration of tight-knit communities, leaving individuals isolated and vulnerable. This dislocation creates an ideal hunting ground for traffickers who prey on the loneliness and anonymity that often accompany urban living.

To combat this menace, a multifaceted approach is required, one that seeks to rebuild the very fabric of communities. Initiatives aimed at strengthening families and restoring their critical role in societal and moral development are paramount. Programs that encourage marriage, parenting, and familial unity can serve as bulwarks against the forces that seek to divide and exploit.

Revitalizing faith communities and their role in moral guidance and social support is equally crucial. These communities can offer a sanctuary for the vulnerable, a place of education on the values that protect against exploitation, and a rallying point for collective action against trafficking.

Furthermore, economic policies that prioritize human dignity over mere profit, that recognize the value of each person above their labor, must be championed. Creating economic environments where opportunities for legitimate, dignified work are accessible to all will help undercut the supply lines of trafficking networks.

Education plays a key role in this fight. Schools and universities must be proactive in educating students about the realities of trafficking, equipping them with the knowledge and moral discernment to recognize and resist exploitation. This educational effort should extend beyond academic institutions, embedding itself in community programs, religious institutions, and through media campaigns.

Law enforcement and legal frameworks must be fortified to tackle the complexities of human trafficking. A community-oriented policing model, one that builds trust within communities and encourages cooperation, can be instrumental in identifying and rescuing victims. Strengthening laws and their enforcement, both domestically and internationally, will deter traffickers and protect the vulnerable.

Above all, a cultural shift is needed—a return to a communal way of life that values the traditional family, champions moral absolutes, and places human dignity at its core. It is only through a collective moral awakening that the tide of human trafficking can be stemmed, healing the fractures within our communities and restoring the sanctity of human life.

In conclusion, the breakdown of communities, fueled by the erosion of family structures, diminishing religious influence, and a culture of moral relativism, has significantly contributed to the proliferation of human trafficking. As societies, we must recognize the magnitude of this crisis and come together to address the root causes. In doing so, we honor our shared humanity and take a stand against the exploitation of our most vulnerable members.

Chapter 7: Unraveling the Impact of Abortion

As we wade into the contentious waters of abortion's impact on society, it's crucial to approach this topic with a balanced yet firm perspective. The act of abortion, beyond its surface-level political and legal battles, drills down into the very core of what we hold dear in Judeo-Christian values — the sanctity of life. This chapter endeavors to dissect the intricate web of societal implications that abortion weaves, leaning heavily on statistical analysis and moral philosophy to guide our understanding.

The statistical landscape surrounding abortion reveals stark realities. Studies indicate a profound effect on population demographics, with millions of lives aborted that would have significantly altered the societal fabric. The ripple effects of such a demographic shift are far-reaching, extending into economic, social, and moral realms.

Abortion's contribution to the devaluation of life cannot be understated. In societies where abortion becomes a norm, the intrinsic value assigned to life begins to erode. This devaluation is not confined to the unborn; it permeates attitudes towards the elderly, the disabled, and any group deemed inconvenient or unproductive by prevailing standards.

The moral quandary posed by abortion extends beyond individual choice, anchoring itself in the collective consciousness of our society. It asks us to consider what values we prioritize and the kind of society we wish to cultivate. Are we inclined towards convenience and autonomy at any cost, or do we value every life as sacred and worthy of protection?

From a sociological standpoint, the normalization of abortion is linked to broader shifts away from traditional family structures. It aligns with increasing divorce rates, single-parent households, and the redefinition of family roles. Each of these trends reflects a move away from the stability and societal cohesion traditionally offered by family units.

Politically, the issue of abortion has polarized communities and directed legislative agendas. Laws reflect and shape social norms; thus, the manner in which abortion is legislated deeply influences societal attitudes towards life and morality. The legal battles over abortion not only delineate what is allowable but also signal what is considered morally acceptable within a society.

For the practicing Roman Catholic, the church's teachings provide clear guidance on the sanctity of life from conception. This religious perspective informs the moral compass of millions, dictating a staunch opposition to abortion under any circumstance. It underscores the belief in a transcendent moral order that supersedes individual autonomy.

Statistical analysis further reveals abortion's selective impact on demographics, with disproportionate numbers seen in certain communities. This raises additional ethical concerns about societal inequality and the targeting of vulnerable populations.

The philosophical ramifications of abortion touch upon fundamental questions of existence, rights, and moral duty. It compels society to delineate where the right to life begins and the extent of an individual's autonomy over their body. The resolution of these questions profoundly shapes the ethical landscape of our communities.

Law enforcement and legal practitioners find themselves at the intersection of the moral and legal dimensions of abortion. Their role in upholding laws that may conflict with personal ethical beliefs adds another layer of complexity to this multifaceted issue.

Legislators tasked with navigating the abortion debate must balance ethical imperatives with political realities. The laws they craft or uphold weave the fabric of societal norms, crafting a legacy of either life-affirmation or life-negation.

Community activists, operating on the frontline of societal change, wield significant power in shaping public discourse on abortion. Their campaigns, whether pro-life or pro-choice, significantly influence public opinion and thus the moral direction of society.

Despite the divisive nature of the abortion debate, it's crucial to engage in these discussions with compassion and empathy. Recognizing the profound personal dilemmas faced by individuals considering abortion, while also asserting the societal and moral costs, allows for a more nuanced and productive conversation.

In conclusion, the impact of abortion on society is deep and varied. It challenges us to consider the value we place on life, the role of family, and the moral direction of our communities. As we strive towards a society that honors Judeo-Christian values, understanding and addressing the complex implications of abortion is indispensable.

Our journey through the tangled impact of abortion reflects a broader quest for moral clarity and societal health. The paths we choose, driven by our collective moral convictions, will shape the future of our culture and the legacy we leave for generations to come.

Statistical Analysis and Societal Implications

In the exploration of the impact of abortion on society, a rigorous statistical analysis unveils a multifaceted web of consequences that extend beyond the immediate individuals involved. The realm of statistics is not merely about numbers but embodies the stories of communities, families, and future generations. When dissecting the societal implications of abortion, we observe not only a decrease in birth rates but a profound alteration in the demographic makeup, economic conditions, and psychological health of a society.

Abortion, often presented as a component of reproductive health, carries with it deep societal fissures. Studies indicate an association between high abortion rates and an array of negative psychological outcomes for women, including increased risks of depression, anxiety, and substance abuse. These outcomes, in turn, spill over into the broader societal fabric, affecting family stability and community well-being.

The economic implications of abortion are equally significant. From a cliodynamic perspective, the demographic changes induced by large-scale abortion practices can lead to a decreased labor force, shifting the economic balance. Some economists argue that the long-term effects include challenges in sustaining pension systems and a reduction in economic innovation and growth (Grant et al., 2014).

Moreover, the statistical underpinnings of societal structure highlight a disturbing trend: a correlation between abortion rates and weakened familial bonds. As the value placed on potential life diminishes, so too does the intrinsic value attributed to familial relationships, leading to a society that increasingly prioritizes individualism over communal responsibility (Everett, 2018).

One cannot ignore the ethical implications of abortion statistics. The sheer number of abortions carried out annually raises profound moral questions about the sanctity of life and the role of societal norms in protecting the vulnerable. These ethical considerations touch upon the heart of Judeo-Christian values – the inherent worth and dignity of every human being.

Furthermore, an analysis of abortion's societal implications reveals a gendered dimension, disproportionately affecting women not only physically but also emotionally and economically. This phenomenon underscores the complexity of abortion's impact, intertwining with issues of gender inequality and social justice.

The societal implications of abortion extend to the political arena, where abortion statistics often become a focal point of heated debates. The polarization surrounding the issue reflects deeper ideological divides, challenging the cohesion of society. It's a testament to the power of statistical narratives in shaping public policy and societal norms.

From a sociological perspective, the normalization of abortion has ramifications for societal attitudes towards life and death, influencing cultural narratives and individual identity formation. The perception of abortion as a choice reflects and reinforces broader societal shifts towards relativism, challenging the traditional moral frameworks that have guided civilizations for millennia.

Statistically speaking, the reduction in birth rates due to abortion has demographic implications, contributing to an aging population and creating imbalances that will affect future generations. The long-term sustainability of social support systems, healthcare, and economic growth are all at stake, underscoring the need for a comprehensive understanding of abortion's impact.

Education plays a crucial role in addressing the societal implications of abortion. Informing individuals about the statistical realities and potential consequences can foster a more nuanced dialogue and encourage responsible decision-making rooted in moral and ethical considerations.

Community engagement and support networks are vital in mitigating the societal implications of abortion. By providing resources, counseling, and alternatives, communities can offer meaningful support to individuals facing difficult decisions, promoting a culture of life and respect.

The statistical analysis of abortion's impact is a poignant reminder of the interconnectedness of individual choices and societal health. Every abortion statistic represents a choice that reverberates through families, communities, and nations, shaping the future moral landscape.

In conclusion, statistical analysis reveals that abortion's societal implications are profound and far-reaching, touching upon demographic trends, economic conditions, psychological health, ethical considerations, and the very fabric of society. Embracing a holistic view grounded in Judeo-Christian values and moral absolutes is essential for addressing the complex challenges posed by abortion and fostering a culture that cherishes life in all its stages.

Abortion and the Devaluation of Life

The conversation around abortion is deeply intertwined with our societal views on the value of life. This critical analysis seeks to explore how the prevalence of abortion has contributed to a broader devaluation of life within modern societies. At the heart of this discussion is a fundamental belief, held by many, that life is sacred from its inception. Yet, as abortion becomes more common, it raises the question: has it also played a role in altering how we value life itself?

Statistics indicate a staggering number of abortions globally, a fact that can't help but shape societal attitudes towards life (Nelson, 2020). With millions of procedures carried out annually, the sheer scale has implications not only on demographic patterns but also on the philosophical underpinnings of our morality. These numbers aren't just figures; they represent a shift in societal norms and values, subtly eroding the sanctity of life that has been a cornerstone of Judeo-Christian ethics.

The philosophical perspective offers a lens through which to examine the implications of such practices. Life, as a fundamental value, has historically been protected and revered. This reverence is deeply embedded in the moral codes derived from Judeo-Christian ethics, which have significantly influenced

Western civilization. However, the normalization of abortion challenges this reverence, introducing a utilitarian approach to life, where its value is measured and weighed against convenience and personal autonomy.

Scientific advancements have blurred the lines even further, offering early glimpses into the womb through ultrasound technology, thereby humanizing the fetus. Yet, paradoxically, this has not universally fortified the anti-abortion stance. Instead, it has led to more nuanced debates about when life begins and what criteria make life valuable. This scientific perspective, while enlightening, has inadvertently contributed to the complex discourse on abortion, complicating our societal views on life.

Sociologically, the prevalence of abortion reflects and reinforces a shift in the collective consciousness toward a more individualistic viewpoint, placing personal choice above the inherent value of life. This shift is indicative of a broader societal trend toward secularization and away from traditional moral constraints. The erosion of these constraints has opened the door to a reevaluation of life's value, placing it on a subjective spectrum rather than an objective standard.

From an ethical standpoint, the justifications for abortion often hinge on considerations of women's rights and bodily autonomy.

While these are valid and important issues, they also intersect with the ethical dilemma of the rights of the unborn. This intersection creates a moral conflict that challenges the absoluteness with which life's value was once regarded. It introduces a competing set of values that must be balanced, often resulting in contentious discourse.

Statistical analyses reveal a correlation between societal attitudes toward abortion and broader trends of moral relativism (Nelson, 2020). As societies become more accepting of abortion, there appears to be a concurrent softening in attitudes toward various forms of moral absolutism, including the sanctity of life. This correlation suggests that the practice of abortion does not exist in a vacuum but is a part of a larger cultural shift towards relativism.

Politically, the debate over abortion has become a litmus test for broader ideological divides, overshadowing the core issue at hand—the value of life. This politicization distracts from a meaningful engagement with the ethical dilemmas it poses, further entrenching the practices without addressing the underlying moral questions.

The impact on the traditional family structure cannot be overstated. Abortion, by its very nature, alters the composition of families, often with profound emotional and psychological effects on those involved. This change affects not only the immediate family but also influences societal perceptions of the family unit's value and stability.

In light of these considerations, a critical question arises: how can societies that increasingly endorse abortion reconcile this stance with a commitment to the value of life? The challenge lies in navigating the complex interplay between individual rights and communal values, autonomy, and responsibility. It requires engaging with these difficult questions from a place of compassion and empathy, acknowledging the profound moral and ethical implications.

Educationally, there's an urgent need to address the philosophical, ethical, and societal dimensions of abortion in a nuanced manner. By fostering a comprehensive understanding of the issue, individuals can make informed decisions that consider both personal freedoms and the intrinsic value of life. This education must extend beyond mere statistics and legal debates, delving into the moral fabric of our society.

Activism on both sides of the abortion debate often reflects the highest and lowest points of our democratic engagement. While it is crucial for voices to be heard, it is equally important for these discussions to be grounded in respect for life in all its forms. The challenge lies in advocating for one's beliefs without devaluing the life and experiences of others.

In conclusion, the relationship between abortion and the devaluation of life is complex and multifaceted. It goes beyond the legality and procedure of abortion, touching the very essence of what it means to value life. As societies continue to grapple with this issue, it becomes imperative to reflect on the broader implications of our stance on abortion and how it shapes our collective moral landscape.

The issue of abortion is not merely a matter of personal choice or legal right; it is a reflection of our societal values and our collective conscience. Navigating this contentious issue requires a nuanced understanding of the interplay between individual autonomy and the sanctity of life, urging societies to reexamine the fundamental values that underpin our moral and ethical frameworks.

The Consequences of Contraception

As society embarks on a journey through the technological landscape, it encounters complex questions concerning the moral implications of its advancements. In the realm of human reproduction, contraception stands as a significant point of contention, presenting a myriad of societal repercussions that demand careful examination. This chapter seeks to explore the multifaceted consequences of contraception, shedding light on the intricate web of effects it weaves across the cultural and societal fabric.

The introduction of contraceptive methods marked a pivotal moment in history, creating a rift between the act of procreation and the pleasures of sexual intimacy. This division, while celebrated for facilitating personal freedom and autonomy, concurrently stirred an array of ethical and moral quandaries. It's imperative to delve into the ramifications of this division, not merely from a perspective of individual rights, but from the vantage point of societal health and continuity.

Within the framework of Judeo-Christian values, the essence of marriage and procreation is intertwined with spiritual and communal obligations. The act of separating pleasure from procreation via contraception is viewed not merely as a personal choice but as a societal phenomenon that bears weight on the collective moral compass. This viewpoint posits that contraception, by design, undermines the sanctity of marital union and detracts from the divine purpose of sexual relations.

Scientifically, the usage of contraception has been linked to significant demographic shifts. Notably, countries with widespread contraceptive use have observed declining birth rates, leading to aging populations and the subsequent economic and social challenges (National Bureau of Economic Research, 2020). These demographic trends are not mere statistical anomalies; they shape the future landscape of nations, influencing policies on immigration, economy, and social welfare systems.

Furthermore, the pervasive availability of contraception has contributed to a transformation in sexual norms. The decoupling of sex from procreation has endorsed a culture inclined towards casual sexual encounters, potentially eroding the foundation of long-term, committed relationships. This cultural shift toward instant gratification and the diminishing emphasis on commitment and responsibility in relationships can be linked to broader societal issues, including the rise in single-parent families and the subsequent impact on child development and social stability.

From a philosophical standpoint, the essence of human freedom is intrinsically linked to the notion of responsibility. Contraception, in many ways, represents the pursuit of freedom devoid of its counterpart, responsibility. This imbalance raises profound questions about the nature of freedom itself, questioning whether true liberty can exist in the absence of accountability and consequence.

The reliance on contraception also impacts interpersonal relationships, altering the dynamics of trust and mutual respect. The promise of consequence-free intimacy, while alluring, may inadvertently diminish the depth and significance of sexual relations, reducing what could be an expression of profound love and commitment to a mere act of physical pleasure.

Societal acceptance of contraception has further implications for the perception of life and the inherent value placed on potential human existence. The convenience offered by contraceptive methods fosters a utilitarian approach to procreation, where the potential for life is weighed against personal convenience and desires. This perspective, subtly but unmistakably, influences societal attitudes towards other areas of life and ethics, including issues like abortion, euthanasia, and the care of the elderly and disabled.

In the context of public health, contraception presents a paradox. While it contributes to the prevention of unintended pregnancies and the spread of sexually transmitted infections, it simultaneously engenders a false sense of security that may encourage risky sexual behaviors. The complexity of this dual nature underscores the need for a balanced discourse surrounding contraceptive use, one that acknowledges both its benefits and its potential drawbacks.

The influence of contraception on gender roles and expectations is profound. By liberating women from the immediate consequences of sexual activity, contraception has played a pivotal role in shaping modern feminism and gender dynamics. However, this liberation also brings to light questions about the distribution of responsibility and power within sexual relationships, raising concerns about the commodification of women's bodies and the perpetuation of gender inequities.

Considering the repercussions of contraceptive practices on society, it becomes clear that the dialogue surrounding contraception is not solely restricted to issues of personal autonomy and freedom. Instead, it encompasses a broader discussion about the type of society we aspire to create. It prompts a reflection on the values we cherish and the legacy we wish to leave for future generations.

Navigating the complexities of contraception requires a discourse that is both compassionate and critical, one that recognizes the individual rights of persons while also considering the collective needs of society. It calls for a reevaluation of the principles that guide our decisions, urging a shift towards a culture that emphasizes responsibility, commitment, and the inherent value of human life.

As society continues to grapple with the ethical dilemmas presented by modern technology, including contraception, it is tasked with forging paths that reconcile innovation with morality. The challenge lies in crafting a future that respects the autonomy of individuals while upholding the sacred values that bind communities and cultures together.

In conclusion, the consequences of contraception are far-reaching and complex, interweaving threads of morality, ethics, sociology, and science. As such, the discourse on contraception demands a nuanced approach, capable of navigating the delicate balance between personal freedom and societal well-being. It is a journey that necessitates thoughtful consideration, open dialogue, and, above all, a steadfast commitment to the values that define the essence of humanity.

Technological Advances and Moral Questions

The marriage between technology and morality has always been a tumultuous one, especially when it comes to the question of contraception. As we delve deeper into this intersection, it becomes evident that technological advances in contraception have raised substantial moral questions that echo the concerns of Judeo-Christian values towards the sanctity of life and the purpose of human sexuality.

With the advent of contraceptive technologies, humanity has been granted the power to control birth, a power that was once deemed to be within the exclusive prerogative of the divine. This significant shift has not only altered the landscape of human sexuality but has also raised profound ethical dilemmas. The very essence of contraception, which is to prevent the potential for life, calls into question the natural teleology of sex and whether human beings have the moral right to intervene in such a fundamental process.

From a philosophical standpoint, the use of contraception could be seen as an affront to the natural order. The Judeo-Christian moral framework posits that every sexual act should be open to the possibility of life. Hence, interventions that deliberately prevent this potentiality challenge the divine intent and the natural law, which guides human actions towards their proper ends.

Scientifically, contraception has brought about significant benefits, such as the ability for families to plan their sizes, which can lead to better economic and health outcomes (Smith, 2003). However, this utilitarian approach to the value of contraception does not absolve it of its moral implications. It prompts the question of whether the ends can indeed justify the means, especially when these means directly interfere with the potential creation of life.

Sociologically, the widespread acceptance and use of contraception have contributed to a seismic shift in societal norms concerning sex, marriage, and family life. The decoupling of sex from procreation has led to a more liberal attitude towards sexual behavior, which in turn has caused a decline in the value placed on the traditional family structure. This transformation has not only impacted societal norms but also challenged the moral fabric that Judeo-Christian values seek to uphold.

The role of religion in shaping moral codes and decisions, especially on matters as significant as contraception, cannot be understated. Within the Judeo-Christian tradition, there is a strong emphasis on the sanctity of life and on sexual relations being a sacred unitive and procreative act. The technological capability to control one's reproductive system is, therefore, a matter of significant moral debate, with arguments often centered around the sanctity of life and human dignity.

Politically, the conversation surrounding contraception is highly polarized, further complicating the moral dialogue. Legislation on contraceptive technologies often reflects wider ideological divides, with some advocating for widespread access as a matter of public health and others cautioning against the moral deterioration such accessibility might engender.

Moreover, the moral questions surrounding contraception extend beyond the act of preventing pregnancies. They touch on broader ethical issues such as the commodification of human life, the potential health risks associated with certain contraceptive methods, and the societal implications of separating sex from its procreative purpose.

The development and distribution of contraception also raise questions about equity and justice. Access to contraceptive technologies is not uniform globally, with significant disparities existing between different regions and socioeconomic groups. This discrepancy not only highlights a broader issue of health inequality but also raises moral concerns about who gets to exercise the power of reproductive control.

Furthermore, the environmental impact of contraceptive methods, particularly hormonal contraceptives, has begun to emerge as a moral consideration. The excretion of hormones into water systems and the potential implications for wildlife and ecosystems challenge us to consider the environmental stewardship aspect of moral decision-making in the use of contraception.

Education on contraception presents another moral quandary. The manner in which young individuals learn about contraception, its uses, benefits, and moral implications, is critical. An education that solely focuses on the mechanical aspects without addressing the underlying moral considerations may fail to prepare individuals for the complexity of human sexuality and the ethical dilemmas inherent in decision-making about contraception.

In light of these discussions, it's crucial for individuals, especially those adhering to Judeo-Christian morals, to engage deeply with the ethical dimensions of contraceptive technologies. This engagement should not be reactionary but rather a thoughtful consideration of the balance between technological advancements and the moral laws that guide human conduct.

To conclude, the intersection of technological advances in contraception and moral questions is a complex and multifaceted issue. It challenges us to critically assess the impact of these technologies on human life, society, and our moral and ethical frameworks. As we navigate these waters, the Judeo-Christian tradition offers valuable insights and principles that can guide us toward a more ethical and meaningful engagement with the power of technology.

Societal Impact: A Cliodynamic Analysis

The advent of contraception has ushered in a series of societal shifts with far-reaching consequences, a phenomenon meticulously unraveled through the lens of cliodynamics. This analysis delves deeply into the multifaceted impacts of contraception on societal structures, particularly the traditional family unit, which has long been considered the cornerstone of civilization. As we unravel the implications of this technological advancement, it becomes clear that the effects extend far beyond the individual, influencing the very fabric of societal cohesion and morality.

At the heart of this discourse is the transformation in family planning practices that contraception has facilitated. Where once families were formed within the context of marriage and children were viewed as a natural and often divine blessing, we now observe a paradigm shift towards planned parenthood, where the decision to have children is often postponed for economic, personal, or professional reasons. This shift, while offering individual freedom, has contributed to declining birth rates that pose significant challenges for societal sustainability and economic stability (Johnston & Hermalin, 2017).

The impact of contraception on sexual behaviors cannot be understated. With the perceived mitigation of the 'consequences' of sexual activity, societal norms around premarital sex have undergone a dramatic transformation. This change, while championed by some as a liberation from traditional mores, can also be critiqued for its role in eroding the sanctity of the marriage covenant and encouraging behaviors that stray from Judeo-Christian values.

Furthermore, the availability and normalization of contraception have played a significant role in redefining gender roles. Women, having greater control over their reproductive health, have been able to pursue professional and educational aspirations more freely. While this empowerment is positive, it also contributes to the complex debate surrounding family priorities and the declining emphasis on motherhood and homemaking as valued roles within society.

The consequential decline in marriage rates ties directly into this narrative. As societal values shift, the emphasis on marriage as a foundational institution wanes, contributing to an increase in cohabitation, single-parent families, and the fracturing of what was once considered the nuclear family. This fracturing has deep implications for child development and societal stability, as the traditional family structure has been shown to play a crucial role in nurturing well-adjusted individuals.

This analysis would be incomplete without addressing the ageing population conundrum. As birth rates decline, societies face the daunting challenge of supporting an increasing number of elderly dependent individuals with a shrinking workforce. This demographic shift threatens economic stability and poses moral and ethical dilemmas regarding the care for the elderly and intergenerational equity.

Cliodynamic analysis also brings to light the nuanced interplay between contraception and social inequality. While access to contraception has been heralded as a vehicle for equality, disparities in access and education about contraceptive methods perpetuate a cycle of inequality, particularly in underserved communities. This inequality extends to the societal level, where demographic shifts impact socio-economic dynamics and contribute to the stratification of society.

The transformation in societal norms around family, sex, and marriage resulting from the widespread adoption of contraception is indicative of a broader trend towards secularism and moral relativism. This trend challenges the foundation of Judeo-Christian ethics, which advocate for the sanctity of life, fidelity within marriage, and the family as the basic unit of society. As these values are eroded, we are prompted to consider the long-term sustainability of societal structures that have historically been anchored by these principles.

To address these challenges, a cliodynamic approach suggests a return to foundational values rooted in the sanctity of the traditional family, the promotion of marriage, and the revaluation of fertility and childrearing as central to societal prosperity. Such strategies may serve not only to stabilize demographic trends but also to reinforce the moral fabric of society.

In conclusion, the ripple effects of contraception on society are profound, touching on demographic trends, sexual norms, family structures, and moral values. A cliodynamic analysis of these impacts reveals a complex picture of transformation and challenge. As we navigate this terrain, it is incumbent upon individuals and society as a whole to consider the long-term consequences of these shifts and to evaluate the role of traditional values in guiding us towards a sustainable and morally coherent future.

Chapter 9: Examining Homosexuality through History

In the tapestry of human history, threads of countless colors represent the spectrum of human identity and experience. Among them, the topic of homosexuality weaves a complex and often contentious pattern. This chapter seeks to consider, with both respect for scientific inquiry and moral reflection, the presence and role of homosexuality through various epochs, societies, and cultures, and its interplay with Judeo-Christian moral tradition.

The examination of homosexual behavior spans millenia, with historical narratives describing same-sex relationships in a variety of lights. Ancient civilizations, although varying in their responses, acknowledged such relationships. For instance, the Greeks, who celebrated the intellect and physical form, often depicted homosexual love in art and literature. Yet, it must be stated that these portrayals were not indicative of a universal acceptance or understanding similar to contemporary views on sexual orientation (Boswell, 1980).

Furthermore, our Judeo-Christian heritage has been particularly influential in shaping Western societal norms regarding sexuality, establishing procreative unions as the foundation for family structures. While biblical texts have been subject to diverse interpretations, traditional Judeo-Christian teachings emphasize that the sanctity of marriage between a man and a woman is instrumental to the well-being of society (Davidson, 2007).

With the advent and spread of Christianity, a transformation in the cultural and moral landscape occurred. Early Christian theologians, drawing from the Hebrew Scriptures, posited that human sexuality had a specific purpose aligned with reproduction and deepening marital union. In this light, acts of homosexuality were seen as incongruent with the inherent design and sacred intentions of human sexuality (Nissinen, 1998).

The Medieval era further entrenched these precepts, often codifying them into law. Such decrees were not solely religious but were adopted by the state, reflecting a milieu where moral and legal domains were intrinsically linked. Same-sex acts were met with varying degrees of sanction or censure, paralleled in part by the shifting attitudes between tolerant and punitive responses to other societal issues (Greenberg, 1988).

As society progressed into the Renaissance and Enlightenment eras, discussion around homosexuality became more nuanced, reflecting broader intellectual and cultural changes. Yet, the prevailing Judeo-Christian ethic continued to hold sway, regarding traditional family structures as the bulwark against social decay.

With the rise of modernity, the concept of sexuality underwent significant transformations, influenced by the emergence of psychological theories and a growing emphasis on individual rights. The late 19th and early 20th centuries saw the birth of the term 'homosexual', a categorization that pathologized same-sex attraction, but which also began building a foundation for the LGBT rights movements that would emerge (Foucault, 1978).

The 20th century was a crucible of rapid social change wherein movements for civil rights and equality proliferated, propelling discussions of homosexuality to the forefront. In the latter half, the sexual revolution challenged traditional mores, arguing for a broader latitude in sexual expression. Simultaneously, the gay rights movement sought to recast homosexuality not as a moral failing or psychological disorder, but as an inherent and respectable aspect of human diversity.

However, this shift has been met with resistance by those who maintain that the sanctity of traditional family structures is paramount. Proponents of traditional morality argue that the acceptance and normalization of homosexuality erode the fabric of society by undermining the central role of the traditional family as intended by divine design. There is an apprehension that redefining marriage may have ripple effects, affecting future generations and societal health as a whole (Anderson, 2013).

It is evident that attitudes towards homosexuality have alternated between acceptance, indifference, and hostility, fluctuating with the sociocultural currents of different periods. Each epoch's stance towards homosexuality reflects deeper narratives about the balance of nature, religion, and society's valuation of marriage and family.

The contemporary landscape presents a patchwork of legal recognitions and moral evaluations of same-sex relationships. In many nations, including those with Christian heritage, there is an increasing acceptance of same-sex marriage and the rights of individuals to engage in consensual relationships with partners of their choice. Yet, this has raised complex legal and religious questions about the definition of marriage and the scope of religious freedom (Laycock, 2014).

Our societies now stand at a crossroads, evaluating the interplay between evolving societal norms and enduring moral principles. It is crucial, therefore, to engage in these discussions with both intellectual rigor and compassionate understanding, as we navigate the delicate balance between honoring individual dignity and maintaining a social order grounded in moral tradition.

This historical examination is not meant to pass judgment on the worth or value of individuals. Instead, it aims to understand how the manifestations of sexuality intersect with societal values as understood within a framework that honors tradition. It is by grappling with these complex historical and ethical dimensions that we confront the essence of what it means to be a flourishing society imbued with a sense of the transcendent and communal good.

Let us proceed, then, with a thoughtful discourse, considering how the historical examination of homosexuality can illuminate current debates and guide us toward a more profound comprehension of the human condition in its myriad expressions, always in pursuit of a society that cherishes dignity, truth, and the common good.

Boswell, J. (1980). Christianity, Social Tolerance, and Homosexuality. University of Chicago Press.

Davidson, J. (2007). The Greeks and Greek Love: A Radical Reappraisal of Homosexuality in Ancient Greece. Random House.

Foucault, M. (1978). The History of Sexuality: Volume 1, An Introduction. Pantheon Books.

Greenberg, D. F. (1988). The Construction of Homosexuality. University of Chicago Press.

Anderson, R. (2013). Truth Overruled: The Future of Marriage and Religious Freedom. Regnery Publishing.

Laycock, D. (2014). Religious Liberty: Volume 4: Federal Law. Eerdmans Publishing Co.

Nissinen, M. (1998). Homoeroticism in the Biblical World: A Historical Perspective. Fortress Press.

Evolutionary Perspectives and Social Dynamics

The examination of homosexuality through a historical lens necessitates an understanding of its roots not only culturally but also biologically and evolutionarily. Within the matrix of societal development, homosexuality presents a paradox in traditional evolutionary frameworks. It does not straightforwardly contribute to reproductive success, yet it has persisted across time and societies. Some researchers postulate the existence of adaptive benefits associated with kin selection or the "gay uncle theory," suggesting that contributing to the welfare of genetic relatives may indirectly favor the propagation of shared genes (Vasey & VanderLaan, 2010). However, through a Judeo-Christian lens, the acknowledgement of such theories does not equivocate an endorsement of the lifestyle choices but rather introduces complexity in the understanding of human behavior.

Exploring the social dynamics, the concept of homosexuality must be scrutinized in context. Societal norms have often drawn from natural law, a principle heavily rooted in Judeo-Christian ethics, where the natural order and purpose of human faculties guide moral judgment. From this viewpoint, homosexuality is seen as a deviation from the procreative intent of sexual union, a foundational aspect of family and society (George, 1999). This perspective has historically influenced legal and moral judgments, illuminating the significant role that religion played in shaping societal structures and responses to divergent sexual behaviors.

Throughout history, social constructs around family, inheritance, and lineage have reinforced the centrality of heterosexual relations. This extended beyond mere reproduction, shaping the very fabric of community and social responsibility. The nuclear family, as an economic and social unit, was the cornerstone upon which societies flourished, often buttressed by religious doctrine that formalized and sanctified the union between a man and a woman.

In contrast, current sociological trends reveal a shift towards individualism and subjective understandings of morality. The emphasis on personal autonomy and self-fulfillment often clashes with collective societal norms that prize the traditional family model. This cultural momentum towards the acceptance of homosexuality challenges the prior equilibrium, generating extensive discourse and legislative changes.

When considering the societal implications of such shifts, the role of social cohesion and the broader welfare of the community must be taken into account. The traditional family structure has proven to be a bedrock for emotional, financial, and moral stability (Wilcox & Wolfinger, 2007). The reorganization of familial norms carries potential risks to this stability, calling for a careful evaluation of the long-term social dynamics involved.

Arguably, the disconnection observed between societal constructs and evolutionary imperatives presents a profound area of inquiry. The traditional family serves not only reproduction but as a vehicle for the transmission of culture, values, and ethics. In the Judeo-Christian tradition, the family is the training ground for virtue, an incubator for social capital, and a bulwark against social disarray. This reaffirms the centrality of the traditional family within the Judeo-Christian moral economy, viewing non-traditional relationships as sources of potential disruption to this cradle of virtue.

From a broader sociological perspective, the historical analysis of homosexuality and its acceptance raises questions about the flexibility and resilience of societal norms. Social institutions have shown both resistance and adaptability to changing cultural paradigms. Where these institutions—the law, the education system, and the church—have flexed to accommodate emerging lifestyles, they reflect an ongoing negotiation between tradition and modernity.

Law enforcement agencies and legislators have grappled with how to address homosexuality, often caught between shifting public opinion and firmly rooted legal precedents derived from

Judeo-Christian ethics. This tension has been marked by legal milestones that indicate a societal trajectory away from these conventional norms.

Cultural activists have also contributed significantly to this pivot, highlighting the potency of civil movements in reshaping societal perspectives. Their efforts have challenged traditional viewpoints, seeking not only tolerance but also the celebration of diverse sexual orientations as part of a progressive social order.

However, any discussion around the societal impacts of the normalization of homosexuality cannot neglect the potential repercussions on the traditional family unit. As the cornerstone of society, changes to its composition and dynamics reverberate throughout the community (Wilcox & Wolfinger, 2007). The devaluation of the traditional family model may subtly erode the generational passage of values that are essential to the social fabric.

Furthermore, the implications for fertility rates and demographic shifts present economic and developmental challenges. The decline in birth rates as a result of changing family structures requires comprehensive policy considerations to sustain population growth and economic vitality.

It's therefore critical to recognize that moral evaluations often reflect underlying concerns about societal sustainability. The applicability of Judeo-Christian moral reasoning in today's diverse landscape is a point of contention, particularly when considering the rights and recognition of individuals who identify as homosexual.

Ultimately, the conversation around homosexuality and its place within society touches upon core values that have defined civilizations for millennia. The challenge lies in balancing compassion with adherence to principles that have historically fostered societal health and continuity.

Conscientious analysis, both empirical and ethical, is necessary to navigate these complex social dynamics. The extrapolation of trends in sexual orientation acceptance, within the framework of Judeo-Christian doctrine and scientific inquiry, reveals an enduring tension: the interplay of ancient wisdom with modern understanding, asking of societies to deliberate the path forward thoughtfully.

In conclusion, while cliodynamics provides a lens to measure and understand the historical ebbs and flows of societal norms, it is within the entrenched roots of Judeo-Christian values and their moral codes that the debate over the acceptance and implications of homosexuality must be considered. It is a dialogue that extends beyond the purview of pure science or religion alone, beckoning instead for an integrated approach that respects the delicate balance between individual freedom and collective well-being.

The Influence on Culture and Moral Norms

The history of homosexuality stretches back into the annals of time, often occupying ambiguous spaces within different cultures. While the current epoch has seen a rise in acceptance, it's essential to examine the profound impact homosexuality has had on cultural and moral norms throughout history, particularly as it challenges Judeo-Christian values.

In ancient times, cultures such as Greece and Rome viewed homosexuality through a different lens entirely. In these societies, certain forms of same-sex relations were normalized and even celebrated, with a stress on mentorship and the education of the youth. However, this early acceptance bears stark distinction from the conjugal view of relationships that resound within Judeo-Christian ideals—a view that regards marriage between a man and a woman as a cornerstone of society.

Judeo-Christian doctrine has significantly influenced the stance on homosexuality by promoting monogamous, heterosexual unions as integral to moral and social order. The scripture, adhered to by billions, unequivocally supports these principles, portraying any deviation as an aberration from the intended natural order. The persistence of these traditions shaped how

Western societies came to frame their understanding of family and societal norms for millennia.

This conception of the traditional family is not just a relic; it has been the very fabric that has held communities together. The family unit, based on the marriage between man and woman, is sanctified as the natural environment for procreation and child-rearing. These fundamental roles have been essential in maintaining structured societies providing stability, education, and moral guidance to subsequent generations.

The advent of homosexuality in public discourse and policy debates posed challenges to these longstanding norms. As movements for LGBTQ+ rights gained momentum, the clash between modern liberalism and traditional values became increasingly pronounced. This cultural shift has had significant implications for societal structure and perception of moral norms, thrusting private matters into the public arena.

Statistics show that social acceptance of homosexuality has grown, with surveys recording a steady increase in support for same-sex unions and rights (Jones & Brewer, 2017). Nevertheless, this acceptance is not uniform across religious and conservative populations, where the adherence to traditional family principles still runs strong. These communities continue to advocate for policies and educational materials that align with their values, battling against what they see as a degradation of moral standards.

To comprehend the full scope of the influence of homosexuality on culture and moral norms, one must consider its implications for the social institutions at large. As the traditional family unit is perceived as under threat, this impacts broader societal functions such as the education system, politics, and law. Each of these arenas becomes a stage where the moral debate on the place of homosexuality in society is enacted.

For instance, changes in the legal system with regards to marriage equality and protection against discrimination signal a societal shift that moves away from strictly Judeo-Christian legal frameworks. The inauguration of laws that contravene the biblically endorsed family structure represent a pivotal point in the legal acknowledgment of different family forms.

The educational sectors too reflect and perpetuate this shift in acknowledgement and acceptance. Curriculum changes that incorporate discussion and normalization of diverse sexual orientations represent a significant move from traditional teachings on sexuality and family life. These changes in the educational fabric have a lasting impact on youth, shaping their perceptions of norms and acceptable behaviors.

Politically, the ascent of more liberal agendas into power can lead to a broader institutional acceptance of homosexuality, influencing everything from military policies to adoption laws. As politicians vouch for and against these matters, the cultural division intensifies, with some advocating for tradition and others for progressive inclusivity.

Community and religious leaders are now challenged to guide their flocks navigated through these tides of change. The interplay between maintaining religious convictions while engaging with an evolving social climate presents a delicate balancing act. These leaders must walk the line between doctrinal fidelity and compassionate outreach in increasingly pluralistic societies.

The repercussions on moral norms are vast. What was once held as an indisputable moral truth is now subject to debate and reinterpretation. This dynamic, fraught with moral ambiguity, forces an examination of fundamental ethical principles and their applicability to contemporary life.

Finally, the cultural perception of homosexuality is reflective of broader societal dialogues on human identity, freedom, and the nature of love. The ongoing discourse raises fundamental questions about the extent to which cultural and moral norms should guide and constrain individual behavior and relationships.

To understand the future trajectory of these trends, sociologists and cultural analysts must continue to engage with and scrutinize the complex interplay between historical sexual norms and emerging realities. This reflection is an imperative to ensure a coherent and compassionate response that aligns with the profound values upon which societies have been built and have prospered for centuries.

Chapter 10: Transgenderism: A Cultural and Historical Analysis

The exploration of transgenderism, its implications on traditional moral values, and its positioning within societal constructs invites a multifaceted analysis. This chapter delves into the historical emergence of gender roles, tracing their evolution and examining the contemporary debate surrounding transgender identity within the context of Judeo-Christian values.

The concept of gender, historically speaking, has been predominantly binary, rooted deeply in the biological differences between males and females. This binary view has not only shaped societal norms and roles but also reflected the moral and ethical frameworks of many cultures, especially those influenced by Judeo-Christian beliefs. The introduction of transgenderism into public discourse challenges these traditional perspectives, proposing a more fluid understanding of gender identity.

In examining the cultural background of transgenderism, it becomes evident that interpretations of gender have varied significantly across different societies and historical periods. However, the recent push for acceptance and recognition of transgender identities within Western societies marks a substantial cultural shift, one that raises questions concerning the implications for longstanding socio-cultural and moral norms.

From a Judeo-Christian standpoint, the sanctity of the created order is paramount. The Genesis account, which depicts the creation of humanity as male and female, has traditionally been interpreted as affirming a divine purpose for gender as a fixed binary. This perspective naturally informs the ethical considerations and moral reasoning within these religious communities regarding transgender issues.

However, the appeal to a strictly binary understanding of gender does not fully address the complexities involved in the discussion of gender dysphoria and transgender identities. It is crucial to differentiate between the theological or philosophical considerations of gender and the empirical realities faced by individuals experiencing gender incongruence. Herein lies a profound challenge for those upholding traditional moral values: engaging compassionately and thoughtfully with the lived experiences of transgender individuals while maintaining fidelity to religious convictions.

Statistics and sociological research increasingly show that transgender individuals face significant discrimination, mental health struggles, and societal exclusion. This reality prompts an urgent call for thoughtful dialogue and humane responses from all sectors of society, including those adhering to traditional moral paradigms.

The philosophical considerations surrounding transgenderism often revolve around the nature of identity and the self. The question of whether one's sense of self is determined by internal experiences or external biological realities presents a significant philosophical quandary. This debate implicates not only moral and ethical considerations but also touches on deeper metaphysical issues concerning the nature of reality and personhood.

In response, some argue that the acknowledgment and support of transgender identities can coexist with traditional values through a principled pluralism. This approach advocates for a society where diverse beliefs and values can cohabitate, respecting the intrinsic dignity of every individual. It challenges both secular and religious communities to find pathways of compassion and understanding that do not compromise their core principles.

Furthermore, the legal and political arenas have become battlegrounds for the rights and recognitions of transgender individuals. Legislation regarding bathroom use, sports participation, and anti-discrimination protections have sparked contentious debates across the United States and beyond. This politicization of transgender issues complicates the cultural and moral discourse, embedding it within a broader struggle over the role of traditional values in public policy and societal norms.

Education and public awareness are key elements in navigating the complexities surrounding transgender identities. An informed populace, capable of engaging with these issues thoughtfully and respectfully, is essential for fostering a society that values both diversity and moral integrity. This requires a balanced education that presents multiple viewpoints and encourages critical thinking about the ethical dimensions of gender identity.

In conclusion, the analysis of transgenderism from a cultural and historical perspective underscores the dynamic interplay between evolving societal norms and enduring moral values. As society grapples with these issues, the challenge for those upholding Judeo-Christian principles is to engage in this dialogue with compassion, intellectual integrity, and a firm commitment to the dignity of all individuals. The path forward demands a reexamination of traditional perspectives in light of contemporary understandings of gender, without relinquishing the core values that form the bedrock of moral and ethical life.

The Role of Gender in Society

In delving into the intricate fabric of society, one cannot overlook the seminal role that gender has historically played in shaping cultural norms and values. Gender, as a construct, extends beyond the biological differences between males and females to envelop a spectrum of roles, behaviors, and activities perceived as appropriate in any given society. The interplay between gender roles and societal expectations has been a cornerstone in maintaining social order, yet it is also a field where significant contention and debate have emerged, especially in contemporary discussions surrounding transgenderism.

The perception of gender roles has evolved significantly over centuries, rooted deeply in the Judeo-Christian ethos that has guided Western civilization. This moral framework posited clear distinctions between male and female roles within society, emphasizing complementarity as a means to uphold social harmony and continuity. Men and women were seen not only as biologically distinct but as bearers of specific, divinely ordained roles that together formed the bedrock of a stable society.

Historically, the division of labor was largely based on physical attributes, with men engaging in more physically demanding tasks and women focusing on child-rearing and managing the household. This division, however, was not merely practical but was imbued with moral significance. Strength, leadership, and protection were virtues ascribed to men, while nurturing, gentleness, and care were seen as the inherent qualities of women. Such distinctions were not arbitrary but were believed to reflect a natural order that, when adhered to, ensured societal well-being.

The emergence of transgenderism as a societal phenomenon challenges these traditional gender roles, proposing a view of gender that is fluid and self-determined rather than fixed and biologically based. This shift represents not merely a change in the understanding of gender but poses a direct question to the moral and social frameworks that have historically governed society.

One might argue that gender fluidity undermines the stability that traditional roles grant society. From this vantage, the complementarity between men and women is not a constriction but a foundation for societal cohesion; it is a narrative that has allowed societies to flourish by ensuring clear roles and responsibilities. This viewpoint considers the erosion of these roles as a threat to the social fabric, potentially leading to confusion, breakdown of family units, and a loss of shared values.

Yet, the discourse on transgenderism and the broader context of gender fluidity can also be seen as an expression of individual freedom and authenticity. It represents a call for recognition and acceptance that transcends traditional norms, advocating for a society where individuals are not confined by the rigid parameters of gender.

In grappling with these perspectives, it is essential to critically assess the implications of redefining gender roles. The pursuit of inclusivity and respect for individual identities must be balanced with an understanding of the broader societal impacts. This balance is particularly poignant in discussions related to the traditional family structure, which has been a central pillar of societal stability.

The traditional family, as outlined in Judeo-Christian teachings, is predicated on the union between a man and a woman, each fulfilling specific roles that together create a microcosm of societal order. The question then arises: does the acceptance and normalization of transgender identities disrupt this order, or can it be integrated within the continuum of societal evolution without undermining the foundational principles of family and society?

Moreover, the discussion extends into the realm of moral education and the transmission of values. If gender is fluid, how do we approach the teaching of virtues that have historically been gender-specific? Can virtues such as courage, compassion, leadership, and empathy be completely decoupled from traditional gender roles, or are these roles themselves vehicles for the cultivation of such virtues?

The broader implications for society are vast and complex. Legislation, healthcare, education, and even religious institutions face the challenge of navigating the waters of gender identity with sensitivity and foresight. The task is not merely one of accommodation but of critically evaluating the long-term implications of these shifts on societal health and continuity.

Yet, it is crucial to approach this debate with both an appreciation for the dignity of every individual and a keen awareness of the historical, cultural, and moral frameworks that have shaped society. The conversation about gender is not merely about individual rights but about understanding the interplay between freedom, responsibility, and the common good.

In conclusion, the role of gender in society is at a crossroads, reflecting broader shifts in moral and cultural landscapes. While the journey towards greater understanding and inclusivity is necessary, it must be navigated with a deep respect for the principles that have historically underpinned societal stability.

The challenge lies in redefining gender in a way that respects individual identity while preserving the social and moral fabric that binds communities together.

In this delicate balance, wisdom and compassion must be the guiding lights, ensuring that in our quest for progress, we do not lose sight of the enduring values that give society its strength and direction.

Implications for Traditional Moral Values

The burgeoning acceptance and visibility of transgenderism in contemporary society represents not merely a shift in the dialogue concerning gender but poses profound implications for traditional moral values, most notably those rooted in Judeo-Christian ethics. The framework of these ethics has underpinned much of Western morality, emphasizing the sanctity of the nuclear family, the binary understanding of gender, and the ethics derived therein. This chapter delves into the multifaceted impact of transgenderism on these cornerstones, exploring the nuances of the cultural debate through a lens that melds philosophical reflections with empirical insights.

At the heart of the Judeo-Christian tradition is the belief in a divinely ordained order, encompassing the very structure of family and societal roles. Transgenderism challenges this order, prompting a reevaluation of long-held beliefs about gender identity and sexual ethics. This shift is not merely academic but touches upon the daily lives and spiritual journeys of individuals, creating a palpable tension between evolving cultural norms and steadfast religious convictions.

One cannot ignore the philosophical underpinnings of this discourse. The acknowledgment of transgender identities thrusts the question of 'essence' versus 'existence' back into the spotlight, a debate that harks back to the days of Plato and continues through the thought of Boethius and beyond. The essence, or the inherent nature of being, stands in contrast to the existential experience of the individual. This dichotomy is at the crux of the challenge transgenderism poses to traditional values: if one's gender can be fluid, what does this imply about the nature of existence itself?

The scientific community, too, weighs in, lending a complexity to the dialogue. While biological determinism once provided a clear demarcation of gender roles, contemporary science reveals a spectrum of genetic and hormonal nuances that defy simple categorization. This scientific perspective, however, does not negate the value of tradition but rather invites a more informed integration of fact with faith.

From a legal standpoint, the recognition of transgender rights signals a profound societal shift. Legislation mandating the acceptance of chosen gender identities in public spaces, from restrooms to sports teams, confronts the traditionalist view head-on, framing the discourse in terms of civil rights. Yet, this legal progression also sparks debate over the boundaries of religious freedom, as institutions and individuals grapple with mandates that may conflict with their moral convictions.

The impact on the traditional family structure cannot be understated. The Judeo-Christian model of the family as a union of male and female, serving both procreative and unitive purposes, faces redefinition. The acceptance of transgender members within families challenges these roles, inviting a broader understanding of love and acceptance, yet also prompting concerns about the dilution of traditional values.

Education plays a pivotal role in this cultural shift. As curriculum begins to include discussions on gender diversity, the tension between academic freedom and religious belief intensifies. Parents and educators face the delicate task of navigating these waters, balancing respect for inclusivity with the desire to uphold traditional moral teachings.

The health care domain, too, is a battleground for ethics. Transgender individuals seeking gender-affirming treatments often confront a medical establishment and insurance systems grappling with moral and economic considerations. The question of what constitutes necessary versus elective treatment invokes broader debates over the nature of health care rights and responsibilities.

In the public square, discourse surrounding transgenderism often becomes polarized, reducing complex human experiences to political talking points. Such polarization obscures the deeply personal journey of transgender individuals, a journey that, at its core, is about the quest for authenticity and acceptance.

Societal cohesion, built upon shared values and cultural norms, finds itself tested by the rapid pace of change. The acceptance of transgenderism may enrich the social fabric through greater diversity and understanding, but it also risks fracturing communities along ideological lines. The challenge lies in forging a path toward inclusivity that respects differing viewpoints without compromising on core moral principles.

The influence of the media in shaping perceptions around transgenderism cannot be ignored. As narratives proliferate across platforms, so too does the power to define norms. Media representation plays a dual role: it can demystify transgender experiences, promoting empathy and understanding, but it can also exacerbate cultural divides, depending on the lens through which stories are told.

Rituals and traditions, the expressions of shared belief and value systems, face reinterpretation in light of transgender acceptance. Religious communities, in particular, confront the task of reexamining liturgical practices and pastoral care approaches, striving to balance adherence to doctrine with compassionate outreach.

The global context adds another layer of complexity. As Western societies move toward greater acceptance of transgender individuals, they encounter both resonance and resistance within the broader tapestry of world cultures. This dynamic underscores the universality of the questions at hand, transcending borders and touching upon the very essence of human dignity and rights.

Ultimately, the path forward requires dialogue—a dialogue that is empathetic, informed, and reflective. It requires engaging with the complex tapestry of human experience while holding fast to the timeless values that anchor us. In this era of change, the resilience of traditional moral values lies not in their immutability, but in their capacity to guide us through the intricacies of modern life with compassion and wisdom.

The journey is ongoing, and the dialogue, ever-evolving. Yet, amidst the flux, the quest for understanding, respect, and common ground endures, underscoring the enduring power of moral values to unite us in our shared humanity.

The Erosion of Societal Cohesion

As we delve into the complexities of modern society, it's clear that the erosion of societal cohesion is a paramount concern. This chapter aims to dissect the contributing factors, emphasizing the decline of moral standards and the ramifications of such a shift. The fabric of society, once tightly woven with traditions and Judeo-Christian values, has undoubtedly frayed in the wake of contemporary ideologies and practices.

The impact of declining moral standards is not a topic to be taken lightly. Studies have shown that societies flourish under a common set of values and moral guidelines (Bove, 2018). These frameworks provide the glue that holds communities together, fostering trust and mutual respect among its members. However, as these standards begin to wane, so too does the integrity of societal cohesion.

A critical analysis of cultural shifts reveals a disturbing trend towards moral relativism, where absolute truths are exchanged for subjective interpretations of right and wrong. This trend is not merely an academic observation but is reflected in everyday interactions and societal norms. The consequence is a fragmented society, where common ground is increasingly difficult to find, and divisions are ever more pronounced.

Traditional family structures, once the cornerstone of societal stability, have felt the brunt of these shifts. The destabilization of this fundamental unit has ripple effects that permeate all levels of society, undermining social cohesion and weakening the bonds that unite communities.

Moreover, the normalization of behaviors once deemed detrimental to societal well-being, such as the widespread acceptance of abortion, contraception, and the blurring of gender roles, has contributed significantly to societal discord. These issues, while championed in the name of progress and autonomy, have instead fostered isolation and a disconnection from communal values.

Statistical analyses have elucidated the consequences of these cultural shifts, revealing correlations between the decline of moral standards and various societal ailments (Bove, 2018). Increases in mental health issues, a surge in substance abuse, and a general decline in community involvement have all been linked to the erosion of traditional values.

It's important to recognize that the deterioration of societal cohesion is not an abstract concept but a reality that affects everyday lives. The weakening of community ties has led to a sense of alienation among individuals, as the support systems that once provided security and belonging diminish.

This erosion is further exacerbated by the pervasive influence of modern technology, which, while offering unprecedented connectivity, has paradoxically fostered a sense of isolation. Social media platforms, for instance, while facilitating connections, often replace genuine community engagement with superficial interactions, diluting the quality of human relationships.

Amidst this backdrop of moral and societal decay, the question arises: what can be done to counteract these trends? The reinvigoration of Judeo-Christian values emerges as a potent solution. These time-tested principles offer a framework for rebuilding the moral fabric of society, emphasizing dignity, respect for life, and the sanctity of the family unit.

Reviving these values in public discourse and policy-making is crucial. Legislative measures that support family stability, promote life, and encourage community engagement can serve as pillars for restoring societal cohesion. Furthermore, education systems that incorporate moral education rooted in Judeo-Christian ethics can play a pivotal role in shaping the character of future generations.

Community-based initiatives also hold promise in rekindling the sense of belonging and mutual responsibility essential for societal cohesion. Programs that foster community service, promote intergenerational interactions, and encourage civic participation can help bridge the divides that have fragmented society.

It is evident that restoring societal cohesion requires a concerted effort from all segments of society. Politicians, educators, religious leaders, and community activists must collaborate to reverse the tide of moral relativism and reestablish a value-based foundation for society.

As we navigate these challenging times, it is imperative to remember that the strength of a society lies in its unity and shared values. The task before us is monumental but not insurmountable. With a renewed commitment to Judeo-Christian principles and a collective effort to rebuild our societal fabric, we can stem the tide of erosion and pave the way for a more cohesive, flourishing society.

In conclusion, the erosion of societal cohesion is a multifaceted issue that requires a multifaceted solution. While the challenges are significant, the path forward is clear. By embracing our moral foundations and working together to reinforce the bonds that unite us, we can overcome the fragmentation of our time and restore the robustness of our societal structure.

The Impact of Declining Moral Standards

The erosion of societal cohesion we are witnessing today can be argued to have its roots in the gradual decline of moral standards. This chapter delves into the multifaceted impacts that this decline has inflicted upon our culture, values, and the very fabric of our communities. At its core, the question of morality is not a mere philosophical musing but a necessary compass guiding the structure and harmony of society.

Historically, moral standards have served as the glue that holds society together. They provide a set of rules and expectations that facilitate trust, mutual respect, and cooperation among individuals and groups. Yet, as these standards begin to wane, we observe an unraveling of the social threads that bind us. Crime, selfishness, and a pervasive sense of alienation emerge, marking the symptoms of a deeper malaise wrought by moral decline.

One cannot overlook the impact that the decline in moral standards has on the traditional family structure. The family, long celebrated as the cornerstone of society, faces unprecedented challenges in an era where values such as fidelity, responsibility, and altruism are increasingly discarded. The repercussions of this erosion are profound, affecting the emotional and psychological welfare of children, and by extension, the future stability of our communities.

The diminution of religious influence in public life further compounds the issue. Religion, particularly Judeo-Christian principles, has historically played a significant role in shaping moral codes and ethical behavior. As society shifts towards secularism, the moral guidelines that once offered a common ground for behavior and law are gradually fading, leaving a vacuum where relativism and subjectivity thrive.

This shift towards moral relativism breeds an environment where the line between right and wrong becomes blurred. It fosters a culture in which individual desires outweigh the collective good, and the consequences of one's actions on others are often an afterthought. Such a mindset not only undermines the societal bonds but also opens the door to various forms of exploitation and injustice.

We also witness the impact of declining moral standards in the realm of education. Schools, once bastions for the transmission of values and ethics, now navigate an increasingly value-neutral landscape. This hesitancy to impart moral guidance not only deprives students of a framework for character development but also leaves them ill-equipped to face ethical dilemmas in their future lives.

The realm of media and entertainment reflects and exacerbates the problem. With pervasive depictions of violence, promiscuity, and materialism, the media plays a pivotal role in shaping perceptions and norms. Young minds, in particular, are susceptible to adopting these portrayed values, adopting behaviors that further corrode the moral fabric of society.

In the political sphere, the decline in moral standards has muddied the waters of governance. The prevalence of corruption, partisanship, and a lack of accountability are symptomatic of a broader moral crisis. Politics, at its best, is a means to achieve the common good; yet, without a moral compass, it risks becoming a self-serving enterprise.

Furthermore, the effects of moral decline seep into the economic domain. Unbridled greed, deceptive practices, and exploitation emerge in the absence of ethical restraint. The widening gap between the rich and the poor is but one manifestation of an economy that often prizes profit over people.

On a global scale, the erosion of moral standards threatens the very concept of human rights and dignity. As nations interact more closely in an interconnected world, the need for a universal moral framework has never been more critical. Yet, the divergence in moral values complicates efforts to address global challenges such as poverty, inequality, and climate change effectively.

The public health sphere also feels the repercussions of declining moral standards. Issues such as substance abuse, mental health crises, and a general decline in physical health can be linked to societal stressors stemming from a lack of moral grounding. The pursuit of instant gratification, often at the expense of long-term wellbeing, reflects a broader societal shift away from values that promote health and vitality.

From a sociological perspective, the decline in moral standards is not merely a symptom but a catalyst for social fragmentation. Communities become divided, not just along lines of ideology or economic status, but in their very perceptions of right and wrong. This division hampers collective action and erodes social capital, the very essence of community resilience and progress.

To reverse this trend, a concerted effort is required. This involves a recommitment to the values and principles that have historically contributed to social cohesion and well-being. It also necessitates dialogue and education, fostering an environment where moral considerations regain their rightful place in public discourse and personal decision-making.

In conclusion, the impact of declining moral standards is vast and multi-dimensional. It touches every aspect of personal and communal life, undermining the stability and prosperity of society. The task ahead is daunting but not insurmountable. By recognizing the integral role of morality in societal health and acting accordingly, we can begin to mend the fabric of our communities, one thread at a time.

Statistical Analysis of Cultural Shifts

The erosion of societal cohesion, a phenomena deeply intertwined with the gradual departure from Judeo-Christian values, stands at the forefront of our cultural and moral dilemmas today. The statistical analysis of cultural shifts offers a panoramic yet detailed examination of this erosion, providing quantifiable evidence of the precipitous decline in moral standards and its subsequent impact on social fabric. Through the lens of cliodynamics, a scientific approach uniting history and mathematics to discern patterns in human society, we can rigorously explore these cultural shifts.

One of the primary indicators of this decline is the change in family structures. Historically, the traditional family served as the cornerstone of society. Data over the past few decades, however, reveal a significant shift towards single-parent households, a rise in divorce rates, and a decrease in marriage rates (Smith, 2003). These trends not only signal a departure from traditional values but also correlate with increased societal issues, including poverty and mental health disorders, illustrating the pivotal role of family in societal cohesion.

Simultaneously, the role of religion, particularly Judeo-Christian beliefs, in public life has waned. Statistical analyses demonstrate a steady increase in secularism, with a notable decline in church attendance and religious affiliation. This decline parallels an increase in moral relativism, a belief system where moral judgments are not absolute but collective societal agreements. The data suggest a strong correlation between declining religiosity and a fraying moral fabric, impacting various societal norms and laws.

Furthermore, the acceptance and normalization of practices once considered immoral, according to Judeo-Christian values, such as abortion, contraception, and homosexuality, have become more prevalent. Statistical evidence indicates a profound cultural shift, with increasingly liberal attitudes towards these issues (Adams & Knight, 2020). This shift not only highlights a move away from traditional moral standings but also raises questions about the long-term societal implications of such changes.

Interestingly, this erosion of societal cohesion and moral standards has not gone unnoticed. Public opinion polls and social attitude surveys demonstrate a growing concern among populations about the loss of societal values and the longing for a return to a more values-centered culture (Nelson, 2018).

Moreover, the implications of these shifts extend beyond societal concerns, penetrating deeply into legal, educational, and political spheres. Laws and policies that once reflected Judeo-

Christian values are increasingly challenged and replaced with legislation that embodies moral relativism. This transformation within the legal framework further reflects the profound impact of cultural shifts.

Analyses of educational curricula also underscore a departure from teaching traditional values, instead promoting a more secular and progressive approach. This change in education not only influences the moral compass of younger generations but also affects societal cohesion by fostering divisions among differing value systems.

In the political arena, these cultural shifts manifest through the polarization of society. Political parties increasingly align with either traditional values or progressive ideologies, using these stances to galvanize support. This polarization, evident in voting patterns and political discourse, further illustrates the profound impact of cultural shifts on societal cohesion.

The repercussions of these shifts are also visible in community and family dynamics, where the erosion of traditional values has contributed to a decrease in community engagement and a growing sense of alienation among individuals. The once-common social fabric, tightly woven with the threads of shared values and mutual support, now shows signs of unravelling.

It's essential to consider, however, the role of technology and globalization in accelerating these cultural shifts. The rapid dissemination of information and the exposure to diverse cultures and ideologies have both challenged traditional mores and contributed to the homogenization of global values, further complicating the landscape of societal cohesion (Turchin, 2018).

To counter the erosion of societal cohesion, some suggest a reinvigoration of Judeo-Christian values and morals. They argue for a return to traditional family structures, increased religious participation, and the reinstatement of traditional moral codes in public and private life. Yet, as the statistical analysis shows, the path to restoring societal cohesion is complex, requiring a nuanced understanding of the multifaceted cultural shifts underway.

In conclusion, the statistical analysis of cultural shifts offers invaluable insights into the erosion of societal cohesion. Through rigorous examination and the application of cliodynamics, we can understand not only the manifestations of this erosion but also the underlying causes. As society stands at a crossroads, the data prompt a critical question: how can we navigate these cultural shifts to foster a more cohesive and moral society?

Amid these statistical revelations and cultural analyses, the challenge remains to rekindle the flame of shared values and principles that once bound our society together. Only by confronting these shifts head-on, grounded in an understanding of our collective history and the statistical evidence before us, can we hope to pave a path towards a more united and morally grounded society.

Moral Relativism and Its Consequences

In the preceding discourse, we have ventured through the shifting sands of societal values and the erosion of stable moral frameworks. It's upon this backdrop that we engage with the phenomenon of moral relativism, a concept that chisels away at the bedrock of absolutes, leaving in its wake a landscape marked by flux and uncertainty. This chapter delves into the ramifications of such a shift, particularly focusing on its impacts on law, education, and public policy.

Moral relativism, in its essence, posits that there are no universal or absolute moral truths, but that morality varies between cultures and is subject to individual interpretation. The appeal of such a perspective in a globalized world is undeniable, offering a seemingly inclusive and tolerant view of diverse cultures and beliefs. However, the adoption of moral relativism as a guiding principle in life and governance leads to a myriad of complex issues, notably the erosion of a shared ethical foundation upon which laws and policies had traditionally been built.

Through the lens of law, the shift towards relativism manifests in a legal system that increasingly struggles with the concept of justice. When moral absolutes are dismissed, the law becomes a tool for negotiation rather than a reflection of inherent rights and wrongs. Consequently, legislation may inadvertently become a battleground for subjective moralities rather than a bastion of equity and justice. This erosion of a moral consensus in legal frameworks complicates the enforcement of laws and weakens the societal contract that binds individuals to a common good.

Educationally, the implications are equally profound. Schools, entrusted with not just the academic but also the moral development of future generations, find themselves at a crossroads. When curricula are influenced by moral relativism, educators are constrained in teaching principles considered universally virtuous, such as honesty, integrity, and respect for human life. Instead, they are nudged towards a neutrality that may inadvertently teach students that all viewpoints are equally valid, stifling critical moral reasoning (Cooling, 1998).

Public policy too faces a quagmire under the shadow of moral relativism. Policymakers, stripped of a clear moral compass, may resort to policies that mirror the prevailing winds of societal opinion rather than grounded ethical principles. This can lead to policies that are inconsistent and lack a coherent moral vision, ultimately affecting the welfare and moral fabric of society. Moreover, without a universally recognized moral baseline, it becomes difficult to advocate for social justice and human rights, which are predicated on the understanding that certain truths and rights are inherent and inviolable.

The departure from moral absolutes to relativism also has a notable effect on societal cohesion. A common set of moral principles and values serves as the glue that holds a society together, fostering mutual respect, understanding, and collaboration among its members. The fragmentation introduced by moral relativism can lead to societal divisiveness, wherein individuals and groups find it increasingly difficult to relate to or understand perspectives outside their own moral frameworks.

Moreover, the subjective nature of moral relativism undermines the fight against intrinsic evils, such as racism, sexism, and injustices that transcend cultural boundaries. If morality is purely subjective, the basis for condemning such injustices becomes significantly weakened. Victims of these injustices can find themselves voiceless, their suffering dismissed as a matter of perspective rather than an objective wrong.

Interestingly, while the intent behind moral relativism may have been to foster tolerance and understanding among diverse groups, it inadvertently breeds a form of moral apathy. When every viewpoint is equally valid, the motivation to stand against moral injustices wanes. People become passive observers of wrongdoings, hesitant to judge or intervene, fearing the accusation of imposing their moral views on others.

In conclusion, the shift towards moral relativism carries with it profound consequences for society. While it appears to offer a pathway to greater tolerance and acceptance, it in fact undermines the very foundation upon which justice, education, and societal cohesion are built. The task ahead is formidable, requiring a re-engagement with moral absolutes that promote the common good, respect for human dignity, and the foundational truths that bind us together as a society.

The Departure from Absolutes in Modern Thought

In contemporary discourse, one observes a marked shift from the adherence to moral absolutes that once underpinned societies, particularly those molded by Judeo-Christian values, toward a more fluid and relativistic understanding of morality. This departure, though subtle at its inception, has gained momentum, challenging the foundational bedrock of societal norms and ethical standards. The consequences of such a transition are profound, touching every facet of life from individual conduct to the overarching legal and educational systems that govern societies.

At the heart of this shift is the contention that moral absolutes, principles believed to be universally valid or applicable, are too rigid or simplistic to address the complex realities of modern life. Proponents of moral relativism argue that context and cultural diversity necessitate a more adaptable approach to morality. This perspective has not emerged in a vacuum but is the product of evolving philosophical thought, societal changes, and the increasing valorization of individual autonomy over communal or traditional values.

However, it's crucial to examine the implications of such a departure. When moral absolutes are sidelined, the very fabric of societal cohesion begins to unravel. Without a common moral framework, societies struggle to navigate ethical dilemmas, leading to an environment where the line between right and wrong becomes increasingly blurred. This ambiguity complicates not just interpersonal relations but seeps into law, education, and public policy, areas that rely on clear ethical guidelines to function effectively.

In the realm of law, for instance, the erosion of moral absolutes has led to contentious debates over issues like abortion, transgenderism, and the sanctity of marriage. Legal systems that once reflected a collective moral consensus now find themselves at the precipice of moral quandaries, forced to adjudicate without the compass of shared values. This not only leads to polarized legal outcomes but also erodes the trust in these institutions to uphold what many perceive as moral justice.

Educationally, the shift away from absolutes has manifested in curricula that prioritize moral relativism and cultural pluralism, often at the expense of presenting a coherent set of values. While the intent may be to foster tolerance and understanding, the effect can be a generation of students ill-equipped to make ethical judgments, having been taught that all perspectives are equally valid.

The public policy arena, too, feels the ripple effects of this transition. Policies that once would have been unthinkable, contravening clear moral principles, are now debated and often enacted under the guise of progressivism or personal liberty. The result is a society that, in striving to accommodate a broad spectrum of moral viewpoints, risks standing for little of substance.

It's important to acknowledge the argument that moral relativism promotes tolerance and inclusivity. Arguably, by recognizing the legitimacy of diverse moral perspectives, societies can become more harmonious and less prone to the divisiveness of moral absolutism. Yet, this overlooks the critical role that shared values play in uniting communities. Tolerance, significant as it is, cannot be the sole pillar on which societies stand. A balance must be struck, where common moral ground is sought in the interest of societal harmony.

Looking to the past, the enduring strength of societies influenced by Judeo-Christian principles lay not just in their moral absolutes but in their capacity to foster community, resilience, and a sense of purpose among their members. The challenge today is not to discard these lessons in favor of an unmoored moral relativism but to adapt them, acknowledging the complexities of modern life while striving for a consensus on core values that can guide societal development.

The downstream effects of abandoning moral absolutes are already becoming evident. From the disintegration of family structures to debates over gender and human dignity, the absence of a clear moral compass has led to confusion and conflict rather than the promised liberation and understanding. This trajectory raises concerns about the long-term viability of a society founded on moral relativism, suggesting that the path to societal well-being may indeed require a reevaluation of the abandonment of absolutes.

Amidst these debates, it's crucial for those who advocate for the retention of moral absolutes,particularly from a Judeo-Christian perspective, to engage with the broader cultural discourse. It's not enough to lament the loss of shared values; the task is to articulate a compelling vision of how these values, adapted to the realities of today, can offer a viable path forward, one that respects individual autonomy while promoting the common good.

The departure from absolutes in modern thought presents both a challenge and an opportunity. It challenges us to confront the complexities of a pluralistic society without forfeiting the quest for a common moral foundation. It offers the opportunity to redefine and reaffirm the importance of shared values in a way that respects diversity while pursuing unity. The journey toward this balance will not be simple or straightforward, but it is essential for the continued flourishing of society.

In conclusion, while the departure from absolutes in modern thought reflects broader cultural shifts, its implications extend far beyond philosophical debates. The erosion of a shared moral framework threatens the cohesion, stability, and very identity of societies shaped by Judeo-Christian values. As we navigate this challenging terrain, the aim should not be a return to an idealized past but a thoughtful reintegration of enduring principles into the fabric of modern societal life. In doing so, we may yet find a way to bridge the divide between the absolutes and the relative, forging a future that honors both our shared humanity and our individual differences.

Effects on Law, Education, and Public Policy

The way we perceive morality and its relation to law, education, and public policy has undergone significant transformation with the emergence of moral relativism. This chapter endeavors to unravel the complexity of this transformation and its consequences on societal structures and individual lives. It's crucial to recognize that while moral relativism presents itself as a liberating perspective, freeing us from the shackles of absolute truths, it concurrently poses profound challenges and implications for the coherence and stability of our legal and educational systems, as well as the formulation and implementation of public policy.

In the domain of law, the influence of moral relativism can be discerned through the increasing difficulty in achieving consensus on what constitutes justice and fairness. As societal norms shift away from Judeo-Christian ethical frameworks towards moral subjectivity, the legal system finds itself at a crossroads. The foundational principles once deemed universal are now questioned, leading to a legal landscape marked by heightened ambiguity and contention. This evolution raises pressing questions about the sustainability of a legal system that lacks a common moral ground.

Education, a realm traditionally tasked with the transmission of societal values and norms to succeeding generations, is likewise impacted. Schools and universities, as crucibles of societal values, are now battlegrounds for competing moral visions. The introduction of moral relativism into curricula has led to a dilution of absolute moral standards, replaced by a doctrine that all perspectives are equally valid. This seismic shift not only undermines the role of education in character formation but also complicates the task of educators in imparting a coherent moral framework to their students.

The sphere of public policy is not immune to the ramifications of moral relativism. Policy formulation, inherently a reflection of societal values and priorities, becomes increasingly fraught as moral consensus fractures. Decisions regarding public welfare, health, and safety, traditionally guided by a shared sense of right and wrong, are now subject to a multiplicity of interpretations. Indeed, policies that once enjoyed broad support are now contested, leading to polarization and gridlock. The lack of a shared moral compass not only hampers effective policymaking but also erodes public trust in government institutions (Cooling, 1998).

This erosion of common moral ground has specific and tangible effects on society. For instance, debates over issues such as abortion, sexual orientation, and family structure have become increasingly polarized, reflecting wider societal ambivalence and conflict over moral standards. The legal system's struggles with these issues underscore the deepening fissures in societal consensus and the challenge of adjudicating moral questions in a relativistic landscape.

The educational implications are equally profound. With the proliferation of moral relativism, students are often left navigating a sea of conflicting values with little guidance. The resultant moral ambiguity does not equip them to make reasoned moral judgments, potentially leading to ethical indecision or apathy in the face of profound societal challenges.

In public policy, the divergence of moral viewpoints complicates the pursuit of common goods. Health policy provides a salient example, particularly in areas like reproductive rights or end-of-life decisions, where moral relativism engenders deep divisions, frustrating efforts to achieve consensus on policies that serve the collective welfare.

This landscape poses significant challenges but also opens avenues for critical engagement and dialogue. It beckons lawmakers, educators, and policy makers to approach the formulation and enforcement of laws, educational objectives, and public policies with a renewed commitment to seeking common ground, guided not by the shifting sands of relativism but by enduring principles that affirm the dignity and worth of the human person.

The call to action, then, is for a rearticulation of those universal moral truths that can serve as a foundation for law, education, and public policy. This does not mean a return to an uncritical acceptance of past norms but rather a reasoned debate about which values are essential for the flourishing of individuals and societies alike. Such a conversation is urgent and requires the active participation of all societal stakeholders, recognizing that the path forward is neither straightforward nor without its dilemmas.

Ultimately, confronting the consequences of moral relativism on law, education, and public policy demands courage, wisdom, and a willingness to engage in the hard work of building a shared moral vision. This endeavor, though daunting, is indispensable for crafting a society that not only tolerates but thrives amidst diversity, anchored in a commitment to principles that transcend individual preferences and transient social trends.

This exploration of the effects of moral relativism is not a call to impose uniformity but rather an invitation to dialogue, a challenge to explore common values that can underlie our collective life even in the midst of profound disagreement. It's an acknowledgment that while moral diversity is a reality of the human condition, society's cohesion and progress depend on our ability to navigate this diversity with an orientation towards the common good.

In summary, the ramifications of moral relativism on law, education, and public policy are multifaceted and profound, demanding a thoughtful and concerted response. Engaging with these challenges, seeking paths to consensus, and recommitting to a shared moral framework represent not only practical necessities but moral imperatives. The future of our legal and educational systems, and indeed the fabric of society itself, hinges on our ability to meet these imperatives with resolve and integrity.

Legislative Actions and Moral Outcomes

In the interplay of law and culture, legislative actions stand as pivotal forces shaping the moral outcomes of a society. The role of law, extending beyond mere regulation of social behavior, intrinsically influences the moral compass of communities, acting as a both mirror and molder of societal values. This dynamic, fundamental in understanding how cultures evolve, invites a thorough analysis through the lens of cliodynamics, offering insights into the cyclical patterns of moral and legal transformations over time.

Consider the legislative frameworks that have historically underpinned societies where Judeo-Christian values served as cornerstones. These laws, often reflective of moral standards rooted in biblical principles, sought to embed into the fabric of daily life, concepts of justice, equity, and compassion. It's imperative to grasp how such laws not only governed actions but also sculpted the moral landscape, nurturing societal norms that cherished the sanctity of life, family, and community.

The impact of legislative actions on moral outcomes becomes starkly evident when observing shifts in laws concerning family structure, sexuality, and life ethics. Legislation related to abortion, for instance, serves as a profound case study. Laws permitting or restricting abortion do not operate in a vacuum;

they reflect and reshape societal attitudes towards life, dignity, and moral responsibility, revealing the intricate feedback loop between law and morality.

Likewise, the legalization of same-sex marriage across various jurisdictions illuminates how legal changes can both emanate from and contribute to shifting moral norms. Regardless of one's stance on the matter, it's undeniable that such legislative actions have played a significant role in redefining cultural understandings of marriage, love, and family, illustrating the powerful role of law as a driver of moral evolution (Lee, 2013).

Analyses through cliodynamics reveal patterns wherein legislative shifts precede significant transformations in societal morals, but also cases where changing moral landscapes catalyze legal reforms. This reciprocal influence underscores the crucial role legislators play in shaping the moral destinies of their communities, wielding the power to either champion traditional moral values or chart new ethical territories.

Adopting a scientific perspective, one notices the predictable patterns of societal response to legislative changes. For instance, laws that challenge deeply rooted moral beliefs often encounter strong resistance, highlighting the stability that traditional values afford societies. This resistance is not merely an expression of reluctance to change but signifies the societal function of laws as keystones in the arch of culture, embodying the collective moral wisdom accrued over generations.

Philosophically, the dialogue between law and morality invites a reflection on the nature of justice and the ends of law. It isn't merely about legislating behavior but about cultivating virtue. This perspective echoes the ancient belief in law as a tutor in morality, a tool not just for keeping order but for educating the citizenry in the virtues that sustain a flourishing society.

From a sociological standpoint, the legislative endorsement of particular moral viewpoints acts as a legitimizing force, granting social acceptance and normative status to behaviors and value systems. This process, known as norm internalization, illustrates how laws can transform private moralities into public mores, embedding them within the collective consciousness of a society (Cooling, 1998).

If one contemplates the contemporary legislative landscape through this philosophical and sociological lens, it becomes apparent that today's legal battles are fundamentally contests over the moral future of society. Whether addressing issues of gender identity, sexual orientation, or the sanctity of life, each legislative action taken is a stroke painted on the canvas of cultural morality.

Statistical analyses, pivotal in cliodynamics, offer an empirical foundation to these observations, quantifying the shifts in public opinion and moral attitudes that accompany changes in law. These statistical trends not only evidence the causative impact of law on morality but also guide policymakers in understanding the probable outcomes of their legislative decisions.

In conclusion, the exploration of legislative actions and their moral outcomes, under the comprehensive gaze of cliodynamics, reveals a profound interconnectedness between law and morality. As society stands at the crossroads of legal and moral evolution, the lessons from this interdisciplinary approach underscore the weight of legislative responsibility. Lawmakers, in shaping the statutes of today, are simultaneously sculpting the moral contours of tomorrow.

As society continues to grapple with complex moral questions, the guidance of Judeo-Christian values, with their emphasis on the dignity of the person, the sanctity of life, and the primacy of the family, remains invaluable. In legislating for the future, may we draw wisdom from these enduring principles, ensuring that our legal frameworks foster a culture that honors the profound worth of every human life.

Thus, as we advance, let the beacon of moral and legal discourse light our path, not as adversaries but as collaborators in the noble endeavor of cultivating a just, virtuous, and flourishing society. May our legislative actions be always directed towards the highest moral outcomes, forging a legacy of integrity, respect, and compassion for generations to come.

The Role of Law in Shaping Culture

In the intricate dance between law and culture, the former plays a pivotal role not merely as a regulator of society's actions but also as a profound architect of cultural norms and values. It is here, at the intersection of legislative action and moral outcomes, that we find the law's true power to shape the society it governs. The relationship between law and culture is symbiotic, with each influencing and being influenced by the other, creating a dynamic that continuously evolves over time.

Historically, laws have often been grounded in the moral and ethical standards of the time, reflecting the collective conscience of society. This foundation in Judeo-Christian values, for instance, has been instrumental in crafting laws that endorse concepts of justice, equality, and human dignity. Such laws do not merely ensure order but foster societal norms that align with these enduring values.

Culture, in turn, is a mirror reflecting the values, hopes, and fears of a society. It encompasses the arts, language, practices, and beliefs that characterize a particular group of people. But crucially, it is also shaped by the laws that govern how people interact with one another and the world around them. The law, with its capacity to enforce certain behaviors and prohibit others, inevitably influences the direction in which culture develops.

Consider, for instance, the legislative strides made in the abolition of slavery, civil rights, and more recently, environmental protection. These laws not only changed societal practices but also gradually shifted cultural attitudes towards greater empathy, respect for diversity, and a responsibility towards our planet. Legislators, by enacting laws that uphold moral values, contribute to a culture that honors those values.

Conversely, law can also be a tool for cultural preservation, maintaining the status quo by upholding traditional values against the tide of change. This aspect becomes particularly relevant when discussing laws related to marriage, family structure, and human life. Laws that protect the sanctity of life, whether through restrictions on abortion or support for families, play a crucial role in reinforcing Judeo-Christian moral principles that regard life and family as sacred.

The erosion of traditional moral values in society is often mirrored by shifts in legislative priorities. As laws become less aligned with these traditional values, the cultural fabric begins to change, often leading to increased societal fragmentation. The role of law in reinforcing or challenging these values cannot be overstated. For proponents of traditional values, understanding this dynamic is crucial for engaging effectively in legislative discussions.

However, the imposition of law is not without its challenges. Legal systems that attempt to enforce morality without considering the cultural context may face resistance. Such resistance not only undermines the law's effectiveness but can also deepen cultural divides. It is, therefore, essential for legislation to strike a balance that respects cultural diversity while upholding universal moral principles.

The case of abortion provides a poignant example of this balance. Legislative actions that either restrict or allow access to abortion have profound implications for the culture's valorization of human life. Laws that protect unborn life are often rooted in moral convictions about the sanctity of life, reflecting and reinforcing a culture that values every human being. On the other hand, laws that permit abortion can lead to a cultural shift towards a more utilitarian view of life, often at odds with Judeo-Christian principles.

Transgenderism and homosexuality present similar challenges for the relationship between law and culture. As laws evolve to recognize and protect the rights of LGBTQ+ individuals, they reflect and encourage a cultural shift towards greater inclusivity and acceptance. However, for those upholding traditional moral views, such legislative changes can be seen as undermining the cultural foundations of society. The challenge, then, is to navigate these changes in a way that respects the dignity of all individuals while also preserving core moral values.

Furthermore, the role of law in shaping culture extends to its ability to deter or punish immoral behavior. Laws against theft, violence, and corruption are not only practical in maintaining order but also essential in promoting a culture that values honesty, peace, and social justice.

It's also important to consider the influence of technology and globalization on the relationship between law and culture. As societies become more interconnected, laws must adapt to new challenges that transcend traditional cultural and national boundaries. This interconnectedness provides an opportunity for a dialogue between different legal and cultural perspectives, fostering a more inclusive and harmonious global culture.

In conclusion, the role of law in shaping culture is multifaceted and profound. Laws are both a product of cultural values and a key driver of cultural change. For those committed to upholding Judeo-Christian values, engagement in the legislative process is not just a civic duty but a vital contribution to the cultural narrative. Through thoughtful and principled legislative action, it is possible to foster a culture that cherishes life, respects traditional family structures, and upholds universal moral values.

As we continue to navigate the complexities of modern society, let us be mindful of the law's power to shape our culture and the responsibility that comes with it. In doing so, we can strive towards a society that values the dignity of every individual and upholds the importance of traditional moral values in shaping a just and compassionate world.

Analyzing Policy through the Lens of Cliodynamics

As we delve deeper into the intricate relationship between legislative actions and moral outcomes, it becomes imperative to employ a comprehensive analytical framework that is capable of unveiling the historical patterns and future trajectories of societal evolution. Cliodynamics, a transdisciplinary area of research that quantitatively studies the long-term historical trends and patterns to predict societal changes, offers such a framework. By applying cliodynamic principles, we can discern the impacts of various legislative decisions on moral fabric and cultural continuity.

The crux of cliodynamics lies in understanding that societies follow discernible cycles and trends, much like the physical world obeys the laws of nature. This perspective allows us to scrutinize legislation not as isolated instances or short-term political achievements but as variables influencing the long-term dynamism of societal systems. Thus, when examining laws related to familial structures, human dignity, or personal freedom, cliodynamics prompts us to consider their effects on the cyclic trends of societal cohesion, moral standards, and cultural resilience.

Key to this analytical approach is the role of complexity science, which acknowledges that societal systems exhibit both order and chaos, influenced by multiple interacting variables. Legislation, when viewed through this lens, is a significant variable that can either enhance societal resilience by reinforcing traditional values or contribute to cultural entropy by undermining them. This perspective is crucial for evaluating laws related to crucial moral issues such as abortion, contraception, homosexuality, and transgenderism—each of which carries profound implications for societal health and continuity.

For instance, policies that support the traditional family structure can be seen as reinforcing societal resilience. The traditional family, as a fundamental unit, has historically been a cradle for nurturing values, morals, and skills essential for societal survival and progress. Legislation that empowers familial stability thus contributes to the long-term positive cycles of societal evolution, as indicated by cliodynamic analysis. On the other hand, policies that undermine this structure may inadvertently contribute to trends of social fragmentation and moral relativism, hallmarks of societal decline phases in cliodynamic cycles.

In the realm of human dignity, legislation concerning issues like prostitution and human trafficking reflects deeply on the societal value system. Laws that aim to protect and uplift the vulnerable stand as bulwarks against the degradation of human dignity, resonating with the periods of moral and cultural strength in historical cycles. Conversely, permissive legislation on such matters might correlate with periods of societal decadence, as depicted in cliodynamic studies.

When considering the divisive issue of abortion, cliodynamics helps illuminate the broader societal implications beyond the immediate ethical debates. Legislation that either restricts or permits abortion can significantly influence societal trends of life valuation, population dynamics, and even economic structures. Cliodynamics suggests that such policies could either lead to a reinforcement of societal resilience by emphasizing the value of life or contribute to demographic and moral challenges reflective of societal decline.

Moving to the topics of homosexuality and transgenderism, it is crucial to examine legislative actions from a cliodynamic perspective to understand their long-term effects on societal norms and cultural identities. Policies that either acknowledge or seek to redefine traditional concepts of gender and sexuality can act as pivotal points influencing societal cohesion and moral landscapes. Legislative stances on these issues may either strengthen traditional moral values, acting as stabilizers in the societal system, or promote a shift towards novel societal configurations, whose long-term impacts are yet to be fully understood through cliodynamic analysis.

The efficacy of cliodynamics in analyzing policy outcomes hinges on the accurate historical data and the ability to discern patterns in seemingly random events. As societies evolve, the applicability of cliodynamic principles to legislative analysis becomes more pronounced, offering insights into the cyclic nature of moral and cultural trends influenced by laws and policies.

Ultimately, the application of cliodynamics in evaluating legislative actions concerning moral outcomes reveals a complex interplay between laws, societal values, and historical cycles. This analytical approach underscores the importance of foresighted legislation that not only addresses immediate societal needs but also aligns with the long-term health and resilience of societal systems. By adopting a cliodynamic perspective, legislators, policymakers, and societal leaders are better equipped to promulgate laws that reinforce the foundational values and moral frameworks essential for maintaining cultural continuity and societal cohesion.

In conclusion, while the domain of cliodynamics offers profound insights into the relationship between legislative actions and moral outcomes, it also calls for a balanced approach in lawmaking. One that is informed by historical wisdom, guided by traditional moral values, and attuned to the long-term welfare of society. Through such an informed approach, it is possible to navigate the complex landscape of modern legislative challenges in a manner that fosters societal resilience and moral integrity.

The Enforcement of Morality: A Historical Perspective

As we delve into the complexities of enforcing morality throughout history, it becomes evident that the task is not merely a legal or governmental endeavor but a deeply cultural one. The tapestry of human civilization is woven with threads of moral judgments and the attempts to regulate behavior according to those judgments. In societies anchored by Judeo-Christian values, the enforcement of morality has traditionally been a cornerstone in maintaining social order and community standards.

The origins of this enforcement can be traced back to ancient texts and teachings, which have been interpreted and reinterpreted over millennia. These documents and doctrines have guided the moral compass of societies, shaping laws and customs. However, the effectiveness and methods of enforcement have evolved, often reflecting the societal, political, and technological changes of the times.

In examining the role of law enforcement in upholding societal norms, one can't overlook the multifaceted nature of this task. It isn't just about policing but about nurturing a culture of compliance and moral integrity within the community. Historically, law enforcement has been the visible arm of a society's moral values, tasked with maintaining order and protecting citizens from harm. However, the relationship between law enforcement and the communities they serve has been complex and, at times, fraught with tension.

This tension arises from the inevitable conflict between individual freedoms and communal standards. The enforcement of morality often entails drawing lines in the sand, deciding which behaviors are acceptable and which are not. Such decisions are rarely straightforward and often contested, reflecting the diverse tapestry of moral perspectives within any society.

The historical record shows numerous instances where the enforcement of morality has led to societal conflict. The Prohibition era in the United States serves as a vivid example. The 18th Amendment, which outlawed the manufacture and sale of alcohol, was intended to curb the perceived moral decline associated with alcohol consumption. Instead, it led to an increase in organized crime, widespread noncompliance, and a societal rift over the role of government in regulating personal behavior.

One could argue that the enforcement of morality requires a delicate balance, one that respects personal freedoms while upholding communal values. This balance is dynamic, reflecting the changing mores and norms of society. In the 21st century, this is particularly evident in the debates surrounding issues such as abortion, transgender rights, and same-sex marriage. Each of these issues challenges existing moral frameworks and demands a reevaluation of how morality is enforced within a pluralistic society.

Statistical analysis plays a crucial role in understanding the impact of moral enforcement on society. By examining trends over time, sociologists and statisticians can identify patterns and consequences of different enforcement strategies. For instance, studies have shown that harsh punitive measures often have counterproductive effects, leading to increased social tension and divisiveness.

One cannot overlook the influence of religious institutions in the enforcement of morality. Historically, these institutions have been bastions of moral authority, guiding the ethical behavior of their followers. In many ways, they have acted as mediators between the individual and the state, providing a moral framework that informs legal and ethical norms.

However, the role of religion in public life is diminishing in many parts of the world, leading to a vacuum in moral authority. This has profound implications for the enforcement of morality, as communities grapple with a pluralistic value system. The challenge becomes how to navigate this landscape, where multiple moral frameworks coexist and often clash.

Education emerges as a pivotal tool in this endeavor. By instilling a set of core values and fostering critical thinking, education can play a significant role in shaping the moral compass of future generations. It can bridge the gap between differing moral perspectives, promoting understanding and tolerance.

Yet, the enforcement of morality is not solely the domain of institutions such as law enforcement, religious bodies, and schools. It also rests on the shoulders of individuals and communities. Grassroots activism and community organizing play critical roles in shaping societal norms and advocating for change. Through collective action, communities can challenge unjust laws and practices, pushing for a more equitable and moral society.

The historical lens offers valuable insights into the enforcement of morality, revealing both successes and failures. It teaches us that enforcing morality is a complex and nuanced task, one that requires wisdom, compassion, and a deep understanding of the human condition. As society continues to evolve, so too will the methods and challenges of enforcing moral standards.

In conclusion, the enforcement of morality is a reflective mirror of society itself – complex, dynamic, and inherently human. It is a task that demands our ongoing attention and engagement, requiring us to constantly reevaluate our values, laws, and enforcement mechanisms. As we move forward, the lessons of history can guide us in navigating the delicate balance between individual freedom and communal responsibility.

Policing and Community Standards

In the tapestry of society, few threads are as crucial as the enforcement of community standards and the role that policing plays within this framework. The balance between the liberty of individuals and the security of the community has been a subject of contemplation and debate for millennia. At the heart of this discussion lies the question of how communities can best uphold moral standards that are conducive to the well-being of their citizens. The fabric that has historically held communities together is woven with the values and mores derived from Judeo-Christian ethics, providing a moral compass that has guided the enforcement of laws and community standards (Bove, 2018).

The policing of community standards is not merely an exercise in authority or power, but rather, it is a manifestation of the collective moral judgment of a society. This collective judgment, informed by a Judeo-Christian moral framework, has historically established the parameters of acceptable behavior within communities. It operates on the premise that certain behaviors are detrimental not just to the individual, but to the society at large, and hence, need to be regulated or curtailed.

The concept of the common good is central to the Judeo-Christian ethical framework and by extension to the policing of community standards. This concept posits that the well-being of the community as a whole takes precedence over the desires of individual members when these desires conflict with the health and safety of the wider society. Policing, in this context, serves as the guardian of the common good, working to ensure that the actions of individuals do not harm the collective well-being of the society.

One might argue that the enforcement of morality through policing could lead to the imposition of a tyrannical rule, where the government dictates personal behavior to an oppressive degree. However, the essence of policing community standards, grounded in Judeo-Christian values, is not tyranny but stewardship. It is the stewardship of a community's moral health, guided by principles of justice, mercy, and compassion that seeks to protect all members of society, particularly the most vulnerable.

The erosion of these traditional values and mores, as witnessed in contemporary society, has led to a corresponding decline in the moral and social fabric of communities. This decline manifests in myriad social issues, including the breakdown of family structures, increased violence, and the decay of communal bonds. The task of policing in such a context becomes exponentially more difficult as law enforcement officers must grapple not only with the enforcement of laws but also with the absence of a shared moral framework that informs those laws.

In addressing this erosion, it is imperative to recognize the fundamental role that education plays in shaping the moral compass of society. Education, not merely in an academic sense but also in a moral and ethical sense, prepares individuals to participate fully and responsibly in their communities. It is through education that the values and principles underpinning the enforcement of community standards are transmitted to future generations.

Moreover, the involvement of religious institutions in the moral education of a society cannot be overstated. These institutions provide a moral and ethical framework that supports and complements the role of policing in upholding community standards. Their partnership with law enforcement can facilitate a more holistic approach to addressing the moral challenges facing society.

Yet, for policing to be effective, it must also embody the values it seeks to enforce. The integrity, compassion, and fairness displayed by law enforcement officers are as crucial as the laws they enforce. The credibility of the police force in the eyes of the community it serves is foundational to its ability to uphold community standards effectively.

Community policing strategies, which emphasize the collaboration between the police force and community members, provide a model for how policing can adapt to meet the needs of a changing society while still upholding core values and standards. These strategies prioritize the building of relationships between police officers and community members, fostering a sense of mutual respect and understanding.

Such strategies recognize that the policing of community standards is most effective when the community and the police force work together towards the common goal of maintaining a safe, healthy, and morally sound society. This collaboration enables a more nuanced and compassionate approach to law enforcement, one that takes into account the complexity of human behavior and the societal factors influencing that behavior.

Furthermore, the role of technology in policing cannot be ignored. Advances in technology offer law enforcement agencies unprecedented tools for maintaining public safety and enforcing laws. However, these tools also raise ethical questions about privacy, consent, and the potential for abuse. A Judeo-Christian ethical framework provides guiding principles for navigating these moral dilemmas, ensuring that technological advancements serve the good of the community without compromising individual rights and dignity.

As society continues to evolve, so too must the approaches to policing and upholding community standards. What remains constant is the need for a moral foundation upon which these standards are built. The Judeo-Christian tradition offers a robust framework for understanding and navigating the moral complexities of policing in a modern context. It upholds the dignity of the individual while emphasizing the importance of the common good, providing a balanced and ethical approach to the enforcement of morality within communities.

In conclusion, the enforcement of community standards through policing is an intricate interplay between authority, ethics, and community engagement. It requires a delicate balance between upholding the law and exhibiting compassion, between enforcing community standards and respecting individual freedoms. In this endeavor, the Judeo-Christian ethical framework provides both the compass and the anchor, guiding law enforcement efforts towards the betterment of society as a whole.

The Role of Law Enforcement in Maintaining Order

The intricate fabric of society, threaded with the values and morals that have been woven through the ages, often finds itself at the mercy of forces seeking to unravel its cohesion. At this critical juncture, law enforcement emerges not merely as the guardian of peace and order but as the custodian of a societal moral compass. The endeavor to maintain order, thus, becomes a sacred duty, entrusted to those who patrol the thin blue line separating order from chaos.

In the annals of history, the role of law enforcement has been pivotal in enforcing the codes of conduct that societies have deemed non-negotiable. An unwavering adherence to a set of morals and ethics serves as the backbone for these enforcement actions. It is within this historical context that the rapport between law enforcement and the maintenance of order must be understood.

At its core, the principle mandate of law enforcement agencies has been to protect and serve. This mission, however, is not confined to the physical protection of citizens from harm. It extends to the protection of the moral and ethical standards that underpin the societal construct. Law enforcement officers, thus, are not merely agents of the law but guardians of societal values.

The importance of this role cannot be understated, especially in times when the fabric of society seems most vulnerable. Amidst the swirling currents of moral relativism, the steadfast enforcement of laws based on Judeo-Christian values offers a beacon of stability. This enforcement serves as a deterrent against the erosion of the foundational principles that have historically guided civilizations.

However, the challenge facing law enforcement in contemporary society is multi-faceted. The evolving nature of moral standards, influenced by a shifting socio-cultural landscape, poses a unique dilemma. How does one enforce a moral code in a society where the very definition of morality is in flux? This question lies at the heart of the discourse on the role of law enforcement in maintaining order.

The answer, while complex, begins with a return to foundational truths. Judeo-Christian values, with their emphasis on the sanctity of life, the importance of the traditional family, and the cultivation of virtue, provide a moral compass by which law enforcement can navigate these turbulent waters. The enforcement of laws rooted in these values not only maintains order but fosters a climate in which the moral fabric of society can be strengthened.

It is also imperative that law enforcement agencies reflect the communities they serve, not just in demographic terms but in moral alignment. Community policing strategies, focused on building relationships and trust between officers and community members, are crucial (Bove, 2018). These strategies not only facilitate the enforcement of the law but also enable law enforcement agencies to serve as exemplars of the moral values they are sworn to protect.

In practice, this means that law enforcement must approach their duties with a sense of moral conviction. The enforcement of laws against acts that undermine the traditional family structure, for instance, is not merely a matter of legal obligation but a moral imperative. Similarly, the stance against offenses like prostitution, human trafficking, and drug abuse reflects a commitment to uphold the dignity and worth of every individual.

Yet, the role of law enforcement in maintaining order extends beyond enforcement. Education and prevention are equally crucial components. Law enforcement agencies have a unique platform from which to advocate for the values that form the bedrock of societal order. Through community engagement and outreach, officers can impart the importance of adhering to a moral code that respects the dignity of human life and the sanctity of the family.

This holistic approach, however, requires the support of the broader community. It necessitates a collective commitment to uphold and reinforce the moral standards that govern society. Law enforcement can lead this charge, but it cannot do so in isolation. The maintenance of order is a communal responsibility, one that demands the participation of all societal stakeholders.

In conclusion, the role of law enforcement in maintaining order is multifaceted and deeply intertwined with the moral fabric of society. It is a role that demands not just adherence to the letter of the law but a profound commitment to the spirit of the moral values that underpin it. As society continues to evolve, the importance of this role only grows, reminding us that the maintenance of order is not just a matter of enforcing laws but of safeguarding the very principles upon which society is built.

In this endeavor, law enforcement stands as the vanguard, upholding not just the peace and security of society but its moral integrity. It is a role of unparalleled significance, one that requires dedication, wisdom, and above all, a deep-seated respect for the values that have guided generations. As society looks forward, it is clear that the role of law enforcement in maintaining order will continue to be of paramount importance, serving as the bedrock upon which the future of societal cohesion rests.

Chapter 15: Education as a Tool for Cultural Transformation

The potential of education as a pivot for cultural transformation is immense, particularly within the context of reinforcing Judeo-Christian values in society. Education, when wielded judiciously, can sculpt the moral and cultural ethos of the upcoming generation, embedding in them values that have been the bedrock of civilizations for millennia. This chapter explores the impact of curriculum choices on moral values, scrutinizing historical trends and gazing into future directions for restoring moral footholds in a rapidly shifting cultural landscape.

At the heart of education's transformative power is the curriculum. A curriculum that is steeped in Judeo-Christian values doesn't merely impart knowledge; it molds character, instills ethical standards, and nurtures the seeds of moral responsibility toward oneself and society. The historical precedent for this is evident in the once prevalent use of Biblical texts and morally infused literature in schoolrooms, which played a significant role in shaping the moral framework of societies. These educational practices were instrumental in forming individuals who were not only learned but also virtuous and community-oriented.

However, the past few decades have seen a significant shift away from this model, towards an educational framework that often promotes moral relativism and negates absolute moral truths. The consequences of this shift are palpable in the erosion of societal cohesion and the undermining of traditional moral values that have long sustained the fabric of society. To counteract this, it is imperative to reintroduce curricula that are enriched with Judeo-Christian ethical teachings, thereby providing students with an anchor in the unsettled seas of modern moral ambiguities.

Future directions for education should focus on developing and implementing curricula that celebrate the rich Judeo-Christian heritage as a source of wisdom and moral guidance. This doesn't advocate for indoctrination but rather for an education that respects and transmits the moral and ethical values inherent in Judeo-Christian traditions, values that foster respect for human dignity, encourage family stability, and encourage community well-being. These initiatives could potentially shift the cultural trajectory, steering it back towards a society that values life, respects traditional family structures, and upholds moral integrity as a cornerstone of societal health (Cooling, 1998).

In conclusion, education holds the key to cultural transformation. By reinstating Judeo-Christian values at the heart of the curriculum, we can nurture a generation that is not only intellectually equipped but also morally grounded. This renaissance of moral education is not just a return to tradition but a leap toward a future where society is anchored in values that have withstood the test of time, ensuring the preservation of the cultural and moral fabric that binds us together.

The Impact of Curriculum on Moral Values

As we delve into the complexities of cultural transformation, the role of education cannot be overstated. The curriculum, serving as the backbone of educational systems, plays a pivotal role in shaping the moral values of upcoming generations. It's here, within the confines of classrooms, that the battle for the soul of our culture either advances or recedes. This section seeks to unravel the threads of curriculum design and its consequential impact on moral values, underpinning the argument with a blend of scientific research, philosophical discourse, and a persuasive narrative aimed at advocating for Judeo-Christian values within educational frameworks.

The curriculum is not merely a set of facts and figures; it is a mirror reflecting the values a society deems important. When the content curated neglects or undermines the importance of traditional family structures, the sanctity of life, and the ethico-moral principles that have guided civilizations for millennia, it initiates a subtle yet profound transformation in societal norms. The removal or dilution of Judeo-Christian principles in educational content is not just an omission but a formative action that gradually reshapes the moral landscape of society.

A stark consequence of this curriculum shift is the erosion of a unified moral compass. Without a common set of values guiding behavior, relativism takes root. This is not merely a philosophical concern but manifests in the tangible weakening of societal cohesion. Studies have indicated that societies with a strong adherence to Judeo-Christian ethical frameworks exhibit higher levels of trust, lower crime rates, and greater community engagement.

One can't overlook the transformative power of education in shaping not just individual character but collective identity. By instilling moral values through curriculum, educators wield the power to fortify the cultural bedrock upon which societies stand. The inclusion of Judeo-Christian values, emphasizing virtues like honesty, respect, and compassion, naturally fosters an environment where moral absolutes are not just taught, but lived (Arthur, 2021).

Conversely, the absence of these values has coincided with a rise in behaviors antithetical to societal well-being. The increment in issues such as abortion rates, family breakdowns, and a general decline in mental health can be correlated with the erosion of moral education that underscores life's sanctity and the importance of stable family units.

In evaluating the impact of curriculum on moral values, it's imperative to discern the difference between education that merely informs and that which forms. The former provides students with knowledge, while the latter shapes their character and values. A curriculum enriched with Judeo-Christian values serves not only to inform the intellect but to form virtuous citizens equipped to contribute positively to society.

The challenge, however, lies in the implementation. In an increasingly pluralistic society, the inclusion of Judeo-Christian values in public education has become a contentious issue. Advocates argue that stripping education of these values has led to moral decay, while opponents cite the need for a secular approach that accommodates diverse beliefs. This debate underscores the broader cultural conflict over the soul of society and the role education plays in it.

Despite these challenges, there are grounds for optimism. Various educational initiatives and private institutions continue to champion the inclusion of Judeo-Christian ethics in their curricula. Their successes have shown that such an approach not only enhances academic performance but also cultivates a more compassionate, responsible, and morally grounded student body.

The impact of curriculum on moral values is profound and far-reaching. It not only shapes the individual's worldview but also molds the collective ethos of society. As we stand at the crossroads of cultural transformation, the decisions made today regarding curriculum design will determine the moral landscape of tomorrow.

In conclusion, the curriculum holds the key to nurturing a generation that reveres life, values the traditional family, and upholds moral absolutes. By reintegrating Judeo-Christian values into the educational narrative, we can forge a path towards cultural rejuvenation that honors the legacy of our forebears while addressing the challenges of the modern world.

This exploration serves as a clarion call to educators, lawmakers, and society at large to recognize the transformative power of curriculum on moral values. As we endeavor to steer cultural transformation towards a renewal of Judeo-Christian values, the pivotal role of education must be embraced and tirelessly advocated for. For in shaping the hearts and minds of the young through a curriculum that champions these timeless values, we sow the seeds for a brighter, more moral future.

Historical Trends and Future Directions

The stately pursuit of education, particularly within the context of moral and cultural transformation, is perhaps as ancient as civilization itself. Tracing the arc of its development reveals a rich tapestry woven with the threads of societal needs, philosophical ideals, and the unyielding human quest for knowledge. This chapter delves into the historical trends that have shaped education as a tool for cultural transformation, and anticipates the future directions this ever-evolving endeavor might take.

Historically, the concept of education was deeply intertwined with the inculcation of moral values and societal norms. In many ancient societies, education was not merely about the transfer of knowledge but was a vehicle for embedding young minds with the cultural and moral fabric of the time. This was evident in the way education was structured around the teachings of religion and philosophy, subjects that are inherently bonded with the exploration of ethical and moral questions.

Fast forward to the Middle Ages and the Renaissance, the role of education in shaping culture and society continued to evolve. The establishment of universities as centers of higher learning became pivotal in not only advancing human knowledge but also in molding leaders who adhered to certain moral and ethical standards. These eras underscored the belief that a well-rounded education was fundamental to the betterment of society and the individual.

The Enlightenment further propelled the importance of education as a tool for societal transformation. With its emphasis on reason, science, and individualism, education began to be seen as a means to challenge outdated norms and foster a more rational and just society. It was during this period that the foundations for modern education systems were laid, promoting accessibility and the idea that education was a right, not a privilege.

However, the 19th and 20th centuries brought about seismic shifts in the landscape of education. The industrial revolution and subsequent societal changes necessitated a reevaluation of educational goals and methods. Education, particularly in the form of public schooling, started focusing more on equipping individuals with the skills needed for employment in an increasingly industrialized world. While this shift represented a significant advancement in terms of literacy and workforce preparedness, it also subtly began to erode the emphasis on education as a means of moral and cultural transmission.

Entering the contemporary era, the rapid pace of globalization and technological advancement has further transformed the educational landscape. On one hand, the democratization of access to information via the internet has created unprecedented opportunities for learning and cultural exchange. On the other, it has also posed challenges in terms of maintaining coherent educational strategies that can effectively contribute to the cultivation of moral values and cultural identity in the face of a rapidly changing world.

Looking to the future, it is imperative that educators and policymakers rekindle education's role as a potent tool for cultural transformation. This entails a steadfast commitment to integrating moral and ethical instruction into the curriculum, not as ancillary subjects but as core components of the educational experience. Emphasizing critical thinking, empathy, and ethical reasoning in teaching methodologies can cultivate a generation that not only excels academically but is also morally grounded and culturally aware.

Moreover, the advent of artificial intelligence and other technological advances presents both challenges and opportunities. The educational systems must adapt to prepare students for a future where technology plays an even more significant role, without losing sight of the human values and moral principles that underpin a cohesive and just society.

In this light, the future of education as a tool for cultural transformation looks both promising and demanding. It calls for an innovative approach that seamlessly blends the wisdom of traditional moral teachings with the demands of a fast-paced, technologically driven world. This balance is crucial for developing informed, ethical, and culturally sensitive individuals who can navigate the complexities of the 21st century while contributing positively to society.

Thus, the directive for future educational endeavors is clear: to forge an educational paradigm that respects and promotes the inherent dignity of the individual, upholds fundamental moral truths, and fosters a deep sense of cultural identity and cohesion. This vision for education is not merely aspirational but a necessary pursuit for societies aiming to thrive amidst the challenges and opportunities of an ever-evolving world landscape.

In conclusion, the journey of education as a tool for cultural transformation is ongoing. It is a pivotal force that has shaped, and will continue to shape, the moral and cultural contours of society. As history unfolds, it remains the task of educators, policymakers, and society at large to ensure that education fulfills this noble and essential role.

Chapter 16: Activism and Its Role in Shaping Public Opinion

The intersection of activism and public opinion forms a dynamic space where culture and values are both contested and disseminated. In this chapter, we explore the multifaceted role that activism plays in molding the public sphere, particularly through the lens of promoting Judeo-Christian values. Activism, in its essence, represents the collective efforts of individuals and groups to advocate for change or to uphold certain principles within society. Its impact on public opinion cannot be overstated, as it often catalyzes dialogue, debate, and, ultimately, transformation within the communal moral compass.

Historically, the influence of community activists in shaping public opinion has been profound. Through organized campaigns, public demonstrations, and engaging discourse, activists have managed to bring critical issues to the forefront of societal consciousness. Their endeavors illuminate the significance of moral and ethical considerations in public life, thereby nudging society closer to the ideals rooted in Judeo-Christian doctrine. The mobilization of grassroots movements in support of traditional family structures serves as a compelling illustration of activism's potency in advocating for foundational societal values.

Engaging in a statistical examination of movements and change unveils the tangible effects that activism has on public opinion. Studies show that concerted activism efforts have the power to shift societal norms and influence legislative outcomes, thereby redirecting the cultural trajectory. This quantitative evidence underscores the importance of strategic activism in championing the causes that resonate with Judeo-Christian principles, particularly in matters concerning the sanctity of life, the integrity of the family, and the preservation of moral decency.

From a sociological perspective, activism acts as a catalyst for social cohesion around shared values and beliefs. In championing causes that are aligned with Judeo-Christian ethics, activists foster a sense of community and belonging among individuals who hold these values dear. This solidarity is instrumental in bolstering the collective moral resolve, thus fortifying the societal framework against the erosive forces of moral relativism and secularism.

Politically, activism serves as a bridge between the electorate and policymakers, conveying the pulse of the public on moral and ethical issues. By presenting a unified stand on matters such as the sanctity of life and the importance of traditional family values, activists compel political leaders to take these concerns into account in their legislative endeavors. This interactive dynamic between activism and politics underscores the potential of organized advocacy in effecting policy changes that reflect Judeo-Christian morals.

However, it is crucial to acknowledge the challenges that accompany activism, particularly when confronting deeply entrenched societal norms or opposing viewpoints. Resistance, both passive and active, often meets efforts to steer public opinion towards traditional values. It highlights the need for resilience, patience, and strategic ingenuity in navigating the complex landscape of cultural transformation.

In educating the public, activists assume the role of cultural custodians, imparting the knowledge and virtues anchored in Judeo-Christian traditions. Through seminars, workshops, and media campaigns, they strive to instill a moral and ethical framework that guides individual and collective behavior. This educational aspect of activism is vital in laying the groundwork for a society that values dignity, respect, and compassion as its cornerstones.

Furthermore, the role of law enforcement and the legal system in supporting or hindering activism efforts cannot be ignored. The rule of law plays a critical role in either facilitating the peaceful expression of beliefs and values or in imposing barriers that activists must overcome. Understanding the legal landscape and leveraging it in favor of righteous causes is an indispensable facet of effective activism.

In conclusion, activism stands as a cornerstone in the edifice of societal moral and ethical standards. Through persistent and informed efforts, activists play a pivotal role in shaping public opinion towards a framework that venerates Judeo-Christian values. It is a journey fraught with challenges yet rich with the potential for profound societal enrichment and transformation.

As we delve deeper into the intricacies of activism and its impact on culture and morality, it becomes evident that a strategic, informed approach is essential for success. The path forward requires a harmonious blend of passion, perseverance, and pragmatism, guided by the timeless principles that have long sustained human civilization.

In embracing activism as a vehicle for cultural and moral resurgence, we acknowledge the power of collective endeavor in honing the moral compass of society. It is a testament to the enduring strength of shared values and the indomitable spirit of those who champion them.

Thus, the role of activism in shaping public opinion is not just significant; it is indispensable. In a world where moral relativism threatens to undermine the very fabric of society, the need for activism grounded in Judeo-Christian values has never been more pressing. It is a clarion call to all who cherish these principles to engage, educate, and inspire, thereby weaving a rich tapestry of moral and ethical integrity that will stand the test of time.

The Influence of Community Activists

Community activists stand as pivotal figures in the tapestry of societal change, wielding a unique ability to steer public opinion and effectuate social reform. These individuals, fueled by a passion for justice and equipped with the grassroots knowledge of their communities, act as catalysts in challenging existing norms and advocating for a transformation aligned with Judeo-Christian values and morals.

Their influence, although often underestimated, is profound in shaping the cultural landscape. Community activists mobilize local populations, drawing attention to issues that may otherwise remain obscured by the mainstream narrative. Through rallies, public speaking, and social media campaigns, they amplify voices that are frequently marginalized, advocating for traditional family structures, the sanctity of life, and moral clarity.

The role of these activists in opposing the normalization of abortion stands as a testament to their impact. By organizing events, providing educational resources, and supporting crisis pregnancy centers, activists highlight the value of every human life. Their efforts challenge societal indifference and promote a culture that respects life from conception to natural death, as rooted in Judeo-Christian principles.

Similarly, the discourse surrounding transgenderism and homosexuality finds community activists at the forefront, advocating for a return to traditional moral values. They argue that the erosion of these values contributes significantly to societal confusion and disintegration. Engagement in reasoned, compassionate dialogue, grounded in scientific and philosophical evidence, allows these activists to present alternative viewpoints that challenge prevailing cultural trends.

Contraception and its widespread acceptance pose another area where community activists exert significant sway. By addressing the moral and societal implications of birth control, activists draw connections between contraceptive use, the breakdown of the family unit, and the decline of morality. Their work encourages a reevaluation of personal choices in light of their broader societal impacts.

Against the backdrop of moral relativism, community activists stand as bulwarks of absolute truth. They confront the subjective interpretation of morality with unwavering adherence to Judeo-Christian ethics. This confrontation is essential in an age where truth is often seen as fluid, and moral guidance is increasingly divorced from historical and religious foundations.

Activists' strategies are diverse, ranging from legal challenges to educational programs, each aimed at instilling moral values within the fabric of society. These approaches not only challenge the status quo but also foster environments where traditional morals are celebrated and preserved for future generations.

The influence of community activists extends into the realm of legislation. By advocating for laws that reflect Judeo-Christian values, activists engage directly with the political process. Their lobbying efforts and public campaigns play a crucial role in shaping policies that govern moral and ethical standards within society.

In the struggle against the degradation of human dignity, seen in phenomena such as human trafficking and prostitution, community activists emerge as champions of the vulnerable. By shedding light on these issues, activists not only advocate for victims' rights but also call society back to a moral center grounded in respect for all individuals.

Education serves as another battlefield for activists. By influencing curriculum decisions and promoting values-based education, they strive to counteract the secularization of learning environments. The introduction of materials that reflect Judeo-Christian ethics into classrooms is seen as vital to cultivating a morally conscious generation.

The relationship between community activism and media is complex yet crucial. Activists navigate the media landscape to disseminate their message, often contending with hostile narratives. Their adept use of alternative media and social platforms allows for the circumvention of traditional gatekeepers, ensuring their voice is heard.

At its core, the work of community activists is an embodiment of perseverance and faith. Faced with societal indifference and opposition, these individuals persist, driven by the conviction that cultural renewal is possible. Their daily endeavors serve as a reminder that change, though slow, is achievable through dedication and strategic action.

The influence of community activists in shaping public opinion cannot be overstated. Their commitment to upholding Judeo-Christian values within an increasingly secular society marks them as pivotal agents of change. Through their endeavors, activists not only challenge prevailing cultural trends but also lay the groundwork for a moral reawakening.

Finally, the impact of community activists is ultimately measured in the hearts and minds they touch. Each conversation sparked, each life transformed, contributes to the gradual reshaping of society in line with enduring moral truths. Their legacy, though perhaps not immediately visible, sets the stage for a cultural revival anchored in the principles of Judeo-Christian ethics.

In conclusion, the influence of community activists on public opinion represents a beacon of hope amidst the tumult of moral decline. Their tireless advocacy for traditional values in an era of relativism serves as a catalyst for cultural transformation. As society stands at the crossroads of moral ambiguity, the clarion call of community activists rings out, urging a return to the foundational truths that have long guided humanity.

A Statistical Look at Movements and Change

In the grand tapestry of social change, numbers often speak louder than words, mapping the contours of movements that shape the realm of public opinion. As we delve deeper into the realm of activism and its undeniable influence on moral ideologies, it becomes paramount to anchor our understanding in the concrete bedrock of statistical analysis. The following discourse embarks on a meticulous journey, threading through the quantitative narratives that delineate the landscape of sociocultural transformation.

The advent of social movements, especially those striving for the preservation of Judeo-Christian values amidst a burgeoning sea of modern ideologies, marks a significant chapter in the annals of human history. These movements, often seen as bulwarks against the tide of moral relativism, warrant a closer examination through the lens of cliodynamics—a discipline that amalgamates historical patterns with statistical data to forecast future trajectories (Turchin, 2013).

Consider the statistical underpinnings of movements that champion traditional family structures as the cornerstone of society. Data consistently underscores the stability and societal benefits engendered by such frameworks, revealing significantly lower rates of juvenile delinquency, educational underachievement, and psychological disorders among children raised in two-parent households. These quantitative insights not only validate the moral imperatives advocated by these activists but also furnish a compelling argument for policy reforms aimed at bolstering traditional family values.

Furthermore, the arena of religious activism, particularly efforts to reinvigorate Judeo-Christian principles in public life, reveals an intriguing statistical narrative. Surveys indicate a positive correlation between active religious engagement and indices of societal well-being, including lower levels of crime, substance abuse, and divorce rates (Jawad, 2012). This data, albeit indicative of a broader causative spectrum, nonetheless highlights the societal efficacy of religious adherence, invigorating the discourse on its role in sculpting the moral landscape.

The statistical examination extends to the contentious issue of abortion, a focal point of moral contention in contemporary society. Research elucidating the psychological and physiological repercussions on women post-abortion presents a complex tableau of adverse outcomes, challenging the narrative of abortion as a benign instrument of women's rights. Such statistical evidence elevates the dialogue beyond polarized rhetoric, inviting a nuanced exploration of the abortion debate grounded in empirical data.

In juxtaposition to the stark numbers delineating the fallout of certain modern practices, the statistical portrayal of movements advocating for the sanctity of life, traditional marriage, and religious freedom illuminates a path towards societal rejuvenation. Evaluations of public opinion trends, for instance, disclose a burgeoning resurgence of interest in spiritual and moral questions, hinting at a latent desire for a return to foundational values.

Yet, the efficacy of activism is not measured solely by the immediate sway of public opinion but rather by the sustained implementation of policies reflective of these core values. Statistical analyses of legislative outcomes post-activism reveal a staggered but discernible shift towards policies that encapsulate traditional moral principles, underscoring the latent power of concerted grassroots efforts (Turchin, 2013).

This statistical journey does not merely traverse the bright vistas of successful movements but also navigates the shadows of resistance and backlash. The quantification of social media trends, for example, reveals an ongoing battle of narratives, where metrics of engagement, virality, and sentiment analysis serve as the modern-day gauges of ideological traction (Jawad, 2012).

The realm of education, too, serves as a critical battleground for the heart and soul of future generations. Statistical evaluations of curriculum reforms advocating for moral education based on Judeo-Christian ethics demonstrate a marked impact on student behavior, ethical reasoning, and academic engagement, validating the transformative potential of education imbued with moral clarity.

In synthesizing these statistical narratives, one discerns a palpable undercurrent of change—a change that is both fostered and reflected by the activism dedicated to reasserting Judeo-Christian values in the fabric of societal norms. The numerical imprints of these movements offer a compelling testament to their enduring relevance and impact amidst the changing tides of cultural norms.

As we stand at the crossroads of moral ideologies, the statistical look at movements and change offers not just a mirror to our present but also a map for our future. The dialectic between numbers and narratives, between data and doctrine, encapsulates the essence of cliodynamics, guiding us through the labyrinth of social change towards a horizon where traditional values are not relics of the past but beacons for the future.

In conclusion, the journey through the statistical landscapes of activism reaffirms the role of quantifiable insights in sculpting public opinion and, ultimately, in shaping the moral contours of societies. It is through the prism of numbers that we glean the potency of movements grounded in Judeo-Christian values, navigating the complexities of modernity with the compass of tradition and the anchor of empirical evidence.

Chapter 17: The Political Arena: A Battleground for Moral Ideologies

The interplay between politics and moral ideologies presents a complex battleground, where the foundational principles of society are both defined and contested. It is within this arena that politicians and policymakers wield significant influence, shaping cultural norms and molding the societal landscape through the implementation of laws and public policies. The efficacy of such interventions, however, often hinges upon their alignment with or opposition to established moral paradigms, particularly those grounded in Judeo-Christian values.

In examining the political sphere through the lens of cliodynamics, a discipline that employs statistical and computational methodologies to understand historical and societal patterns, one can discern the cyclic nature of ideological dominance in governance. This analytical approach reveals how shifts in political ideologies mirror broader societal transformations, often resulting in legislation that reflects the prevailing moral outlook (Turchin, 2013).

The influence of Judeo-Christian values on Western political systems cannot be overstated. These values, which emphasize the sanctity of life, the importance of family, and principles of justice and compassion, have historically served as a bedrock for legislative frameworks globally. However, as cultural norms evolve, there has been a noticeable shift towards relativism and secularism in the political arena, challenging the traditional moral foundation of societies (Smith & Denton, 2005).

One of the most contentious battlegrounds in recent times concerns the issues of abortion, sexuality, and the structure of the family. Policies that license abortion and transformative gender ideologies, for instance, starkly contrast the Judeo-Christian ethic that views life as sacred from conception and recognizes the biological reality of sex and the traditional family structure as fundamental to societal well-being. Such legislation not only has profound moral implications but also sociocultural and demographic consequences, affecting the very fabric of society.

Furthermore, the legal endorsement of same-sex marriage and the normalization of contraceptive use represent significant deviations from traditional moral teachings. These developments indicate a shifting societal paradigm that values individual autonomy and subjective definitions of happiness above established moral absolutes. While proponents argue these policies promote inclusivity and personal freedom, critics contend they undermine the traditional family unit, eroding the cornerstone of a healthy society.

Politicians play a pivotal role in this ideological battleground, with their policy positions reflecting broader moral debates. The polarization observed in contemporary politics often mirrors the divide in societal values, with parties aligning themselves with either a progressive or a conservative moral framework. The resulting legislation thus not only shapes the legal structure of society but also sends powerful messages about what is considered morally acceptable and desirable.

In response to the moral relativism permeating the political landscape, a counter-movement advocating for the reaffirmation of Judeo-Christian values in public policy has emerged. This movement argues that the principles derived from these religious traditions provide a proven foundation for a just, prosperous, and cohesive society. It posits that policies rooted in these values promote the common good by fostering family stability, protecting life at all stages, and encouraging a culture of responsibility and care for the vulnerable.

Undeniably, the political arena serves as a reflection of the society's collective moral stance and a battleground where competing ideologies vie for dominance. The outcome of these ideological confrontations has far-reaching implications, not only for current generations but for the future societal landscape.

It is essential, therefore, for those engaged in politics to consider the long-term implications of the policies they advocate for. In doing so, they must ponder whether these policies contribute to the cultivation of a society that values and upholds the dignity of every person, fosters genuine community, and strives for justice and the common good.

As society continues to navigate the complexities of modern moral dilemmas, the political arena remains a critical platform for the articulation and enactment of values. The decisions made within this sphere will inevitably shape the trajectory of moral and cultural evolution, for better or worse. In the end, the legacy of today's political leaders will be judged by the extent to which their policies promoted a culture that respects life, honors family, and encourages individuals to live in accordance with principles that transcend temporal trends and fleeting desires.

In conclusion, the political realm, with its inherent capacity to legislate morality, is a powerful force in the battle to define societal norms. As such, it is imperative that those who inhabit this domain are guided by a coherent and timeless moral framework, one that embraces the wisdom of the past to navigate the complexities of the present. In aligning policies with Judeo-Christian values, society can aspire to a future that respects life, fosters genuine human flourishing, and upholds the common good.

Analyzing Political Trends through Cliodynamics

In grappling with the complex interplay between politics and moral ideologies, it becomes imperative to engage with cliodynamics, an analytical framework that allows us to disentangle the threads of human social development and political trends. This approach is not merely academic; it serves as a compass, guiding us through the tumultuous waves of political change, delineating how the fabric of society is continuously woven and re-woven through the actions and reactions of its members.

At the heart of cliodynamics is the understanding that societies are not static. They evolve, influenced by myriad factors including economic conditions, technological advancements, and importantly, shifts in cultural and moral norms. Political shifts, therefore, are not random but are deeply rooted in the preceding social conditions and cultural milieu. This perspective sheds light on the current battleground of moral ideologies within the political arena, emphasizing the critical role of maintaining Judeo-Christian values as the bedrock of societal health and stability.

Through cliodynamics, we can systematically analyze the ebb and flow of political ideologies and their alignment or divergence from traditional moral values. The statistical tools and computational simulations inherent in this discipline provide a quantitative backing to what many observers of society have noted qualitatively: that departures from Judeo-Christian values correlate with societal issues including increases in crime, family breakdown, and general societal malaise.

One might inquire, how does cliodynamics apply to understanding shifts in political trends specifically related to moral ideologies? It's through the predictive capacity of cliodynamics, which enables researchers and policymakers alike to anticipate societal shifts based on historical patterns and current trends. This predictive ability is not about forecasting the future with certainty but about understanding potential outcomes of current societal trajectories.

For instance, the decline of traditional family structures, as evidenced by rising divorce rates and the normalization of non-traditional family arrangements, has profound implications for political trends. Cliodynamics allows for the analysis of such changes over time, illustrating how these shifts in the fundamental unit of society - the family - lead to broader changes in political and cultural norms.

This analytical framework also brings to light the role of legislators and policymakers in either stemming the tide of moral decline or accelerating it. By examining historical patterns, cliodynamics offers insights into how certain legislative actions have either bolstered or eroded Judeo-Christian values, directly impacting the moral fiber of society.

Moreover, cliodynamics provides a lens through which the impact of education on moral and cultural norms can be assessed. As educational institutions increasingly move away from principles rooted in Judeo-Christian values, the political implications become clear through the lens of cliodynamics, signaling a shift towards moral relativism and away from absolute moral standards.

Significantly, the application of cliodynamics to the analysis of current political trends reveals the importance of activism and community engagement. The framework suggests that grassroots movements and community activism play a pivotal role in shaping public opinion and, by extension, political outcomes. This is particularly relevant for those advocating for a return to Judeo-Christian moral values in the public and political sphere.

The cliodynamic perspective also challenges the prevailing narratives around the consequences of technological advancements and economic systems on society. By tracing the historical impact of similar innovations and economic shifts, it offers a nuanced view of how these factors can influence moral ideologies within the political arena.

In addition, global trends, including globalization and cultural homogenization, are analyzed through the cliodynamics lens to understand their implications for Judeo-Christian values. The framework suggests that while globalization has connected the world in unprecedented ways, it also poses challenges to the preservation of cultural and moral norms.

As we chart the course of political trends through the analysis provided by cliodynamics, it becomes apparent that a comprehensive understanding of historical patterns and current societal dynamics is essential. This ensures that efforts to reinforce Judeo-Christian values are grounded in a deep understanding of the forces shaping our world.

In conclusion, the utilization of cliodynamics in analyzing political trends offers a robust framework for understanding the complexities of the political arena as a battleground for moral ideologies. It underscores the importance of an informed and proactive approach to safeguarding the values that form the cornerstone of a healthy society.

Ultimately, the message is clear: as society faces unprecedented challenges, the principles and values underpinning the Judeo-Christian tradition offer a beacon of hope. It is through the meticulous analysis provided by cliodynamics that the path forward emerges, illuminating the way towards a society that cherishes and upholds these enduring values.

The Influence of Politicians on Cultural Norms

In today's ever-evolving political landscape, the influence of politicians on cultural norms has never been more profound. As the guardians and shapers of policy, politicians possess a unique platform from which they can either fortify the societal fabric with traditional moral values or, contrastingly, lead it towards a more liberal and permissive future. This dichotomy of potential paths presents a critical junction for societies, especially at a time when moral relativism appears to be gaining ground.

The salience of Judeo-Christian values in shaping public policy and, by extension, cultural norms, cannot be overstated. Historically, these values have provided a moral compass, guiding legislation that underpins societal structures and behavior. However, as the public square becomes increasingly secularized, the vacuum left by the retreat of religious influence is often filled by policymakers who may not share this moral vision.

This shift has significant implications for traditional family structures, which are the bedrock of society. Policies promoting or demoting family values set the tone for cultural attitudes towards marriage, parenthood, and domestic life. Politicians, through their legislative power, have the capacity to either support or undermine the institution of the family, with lasting repercussions on societal health and stability.

Further complicating this scenario is the intricate relationship between law and morality. While not all moral beliefs translate seamlessly into law, the legal system is undeniably a reflection of a society's prevailing moral ethos. As such, politicians, through their legislative agenda, play a pivotal role in shaping this ethos. The laws they pass not only govern behavior but also subtly endorse certain values over others, nudging societal norms in one direction or another.

For instance, debates surrounding contentious issues such as abortion, contraception, and homosexuality are not merely legal or political – they are deeply moral. The stances that politicians take on these issues, and the policies they enact, reflect and shape societal attitudes towards life, human dignity, and the nature of human relationships.

Transgenderism and its recognition in law serve as another illustrative example. As politicians grapple with questions of gender identity and rights, their decisions do more than adjust the legal framework; they also signal a cultural shift towards understanding and interpreting gender, with implications for traditional moral values.

The conversation around these topics also reveals a broader trend of moral relativism, where absolute truths are increasingly dismissed in favor of subjective interpretations of right and wrong. Politicians, often swayed by shifting public opinions and the desire for electoral success, may contribute to this trend by endorsing policies that reflect a relativistic stance.

However, this approach overlooks the stabilizing role of absolute moral values, which have historically served to bind communities together. As politicians distance themselves from these absolutes, they risk eroding the social cohesion necessary for a thriving society.

Yet, it's crucial to recognize the potential for political figures to act as agents of moral clarity and renewal. By advocating for policies aligned with Judeo-Christian values, they can play a crucial part in revitalizing the cultural landscape, reinforcing the significance of the traditional family, and promoting a culture of life and dignity.

In a democratic society, the power of the electorate cannot be underestimated. Voters have the opportunity to hold politicians accountable for the cultural and moral implications of their policies. By actively engaging in the political process and voting for candidates who uphold traditional moral values, citizens can influence the direction in which their society moves.

Moreover, the role of education in forming the next generation of leaders and voters is paramount. By instilling a deep understanding and appreciation for Judeo-Christian morals, society can ensure that future policymakers are equipped to make decisions that uphold these values. This long-term approach is essential in countering the tide of moral relativism and ensuring the preservation of a moral societal fabric.

In conclusion, politicians wield considerable influence over cultural norms through the policies they advocate and implement. In a world where the moral foundations of society are under constant scrutiny and challenge, the decisions made by these policymakers can either erode or reinforce the bedrock of traditional values. It is therefore imperative for society to remain vigilant, actively engage in the democratic process, and advocate for policies that uphold the dignity of the human person and the sanctity of the traditional family.

The interconnectedness of law, morality, and culture underscores the vital role that politicians play in shaping the moral trajectory of society. As the political arena continues to be a battleground for moral ideologies, the choices made by politicians will undoubtedly resonate through the fabric of culture for generations to come.

The Media's Impact on Culture and Morality

In today's fast-paced world, the influence of media on culture and morality cannot be overstated. As the purveyors of information and entertainment, media entities hold a significant sway over public opinion and societal norms. This chapter delves into the complex interplay between media — including propaganda, news, and entertainment — and its shaping of public perception, moral values, and cultural trends.

The omnipresence of media in modern life has led to its increased capacity to influence personal and collective ideologies. Through both subtle cues and overt messages, it molds societal norms and perceptions, often reflecting and exacerbating the decline of traditional moral values. The proliferation of digital media, in particular, has facilitated this spread, making it more challenging to parse the implications for culture and morality.

Consider the role of news media, which ostensibly serves to inform the public about current events and critical issues. However, the selection, framing, and interpretation of news stories often reflect particular ideological biases. This selective portrayal can shape public opinion in ways that may not align with reality, thereby distorting the collective moral compass (Nelson, 2018). The underlying motivations can range from the pursuit of ratings to the desire to influence public policy, reflecting broader societal shifts away from traditional values.

Entertainment media, on the other hand, often engages in the normalization of behaviors and lifestyles that stand in stark contrast to Judeo-Christian morals. Television shows, movies, and music videos frequently showcase themes of violence, promiscuity, and materialism, subtly insinuating that such behaviors are acceptable, if not desirable. Over time, these portrayals can erode the moral foundations of society, undermining the traditional family structure and the cultivation of virtues (Nelson, 2018).

Moreover, the impact of propaganda cannot be underestimated. Throughout history, media has been used as a tool for the manipulation of public opinion, often employed by those in power to maintain control or push a particular agenda. In contemporary society, this manipulation has become more sophisticated, leveraging social media algorithms and data analytics to target individuals with unprecedented precision (MacLeod, 2019).

However, the media also holds the potential to be a force for good, promoting positive values and inspiring collective action towards societal improvement. The key lies in discernment and critical engagement with media content. Individuals must learn to recognize bias, question narratives, and seek out a diversity of perspectives in order to form a well-rounded understanding of the world. This, in turn, can contribute to the strengthening of moral codes and the revitalization of culture.

Educational institutions play a critical role in cultivating this media literacy, equipping students with the tools to critically analyze the media they consume. By fostering an understanding of media's influence, educators can empower future generations to navigate the complex media landscape with integrity and discernment.

In conclusion, the media's influence on culture and morality is profound, acting as both a mirror and a mold for societal norms. While it presents significant challenges to the preservation and revival of Judeo-Christian values, it also offers opportunities for positive engagement and cultural transformation. The task at hand is to harness media's potential for good, critically engaging with its content to promote a society grounded in traditional moral values.

Propaganda, News, and Entertainment

In the ambit of media's impact on culture and morality, the trifecta of propaganda, news, and entertainment plays a pivotal role, weaving intricate patterns that shape public perceptions, beliefs, and behaviors. Grounded in the premise that mass media commands an unparalleled influence in contemporary society, this discourse navigates the nuanced interplay between these media forms and the societal ethos, particularly under the lens of Judeo-Christian values.

The term 'propaganda' might evoke images of authoritarian regimes; however, its manifestation is far more ubiquitous and subtle in democratic societies. Propaganda, in its essence, seeks to mold public opinion, often by oversimplifying complex issues or capitalizing on emotional appeals. Its presence in news and entertainment is increasingly nuanced, shaped by the interconnected domains of politics, culture, and economics (Nelson, 2018). The challenge lies in discerning the line where information becomes indoctrination, a task complicated by the blending of fact and opinion in contemporary news outlets.

News media, purportedly the bastion of objectivity, finds itself embroiled in a conundrum of bias, both conscious and unconscious. The dichotomy of reporting versus influence blurs as news entities navigate the tumultuous waters of audience retention and digital virality. As gatekeepers of information, they wield potent power in framing issues, a reality that can either fortify or diminish the societal moral fabric.

Entertainment media, on the other hand, serves as a crucible for cultural norms and values. Through its narratives—whether in film, television, or digital platforms—it reflects and simultaneously molds societal standards. The portrayal of relationships, identity, and morality within these narratives not only mirrors existing societal beliefs but also propels the audience towards envisaged norms. It's here that the Judeo-Christian moral compass faces profound challenges, as traditional values often find themselves at odds with the progressive ideologies promulgated through mainstream entertainment.

At its best, the interplay between propaganda, news, and entertainment can enlighten, inform, and entertain, contributing to a well-rounded, informed public. However, the infiltration of agendas and the erosion of objective reporting pose palpable threats to intellectual freedom and moral clarity.

The capacity for these media forms to shape morality cannot be overstated. In a landscape where the absolute is eschewed for the relative, and traditional mores are challenged under the guise of progressivism, the media's role in crafting the moral zeitgeist is both significant and controversial.

This dynamic interaction raises critical questions about the stewardship of truth and the ethical obligations of media practitioners. It calls for a discerning audience, equipped with critical thinking skills, to navigate the mire of information and entertainment. Moreover, it underscores the need for media that champions objective truth, upholds Judeo-Christian values, and fosters a culture of moral integrity.

The propagandistic undertones within news and entertainment often serve to normalize ideologies antithetical to traditional values. For instance, the portrayal of abortion as a matter of choice rather than a moral quandary reflects a seismic shift in the cultural narrative, one that diminishes the sanctity of life, a cornerstone of Judeo-Christian doctrine (Nelson, 2018).

Similarly, the normalization of transgenderism and homosexuality through sympathetic character portrayals and storyline arcs challenges the biblical understanding of gender and sexuality. Such representations, while advocating for tolerance and inclusion, often marginalize traditional beliefs, framing them as outdated or bigoted.

The role of media in shaping the discourse on contraception and immorality further evidences its potent influence on societal norms. By championing sexual liberation and the decoupling of sex from procreation, the media sows seeds of moral relativism, undermining the Judeo-Christian ethic that values the sanctity of marital intimacy and the procreative purpose of sexuality.

In this milieu, the call for media literacy becomes paramount. An informed audience, capable of discerning fact from fiction, and recognizing underlying biases and agendas, is the bulwark against the tide of moral relativism. Equally important is the support for media outlets that endeavor to uphold truth, promote genuine dialogue, and respect the pluralism of beliefs within the societal fabric.

The challenge, therefore, extends beyond mere consumption of media to active engagement with it. It entails supporting creators and journalists who respect the complexity of moral questions and resist the allure of sensationalism. It involves critical engagement with content, recognizing the power of media not just as a mirror of society but as a molder of culture.

In conclusion, the convergence of propaganda, news, and entertainment holds profound implications for culture and morality. In a society increasingly characterized by moral ambivalence and relativism, the need for media that champions truth, upholds dignity, and respects traditional values has never been more acute. As custodians of culture, it behooves us to critically assess the media we consume, support endeavors that align with our moral convictions, and cultivate a public discourse that values truth, integrity, and the common good.

Shaping Public Perception through Media

Media has long been recognized as a significant force in shaping public perception, serving as a bridge between the world's events and the audience's understanding of them. The power of the media, in its various forms, from news broadcasts to entertainment, cannot be understated in its ability to influence cultural norms and moral values. As we navigate the complex interplay between media and morality, it becomes essential to examine the mechanisms through which media shapes public perception and, consequently, impacts culture and morality.

The evolution of media technologies has brought about unprecedented access to information, transforming the landscape of communication and allowing for a pervasive influence on the public's collective consciousness. This transformation has raised pertinent questions regarding the role of media in either upholding or undermining the traditional values that have been the cornerstone of societal formations. The media's ability to shape opinions, attitudes, and behaviors makes it a potent tool for cultural engineering, with implications for the propagation of Judeo-Christian values and mores.

At the heart of the media's influence is its capacity to frame issues, subtly guiding the interpretation of events and information through the lens it provides to the audience. This framing effect, as discussed in academic circles, underscores the power of media narratives to emphasize certain aspects of a story while omitting others, thereby shaping the perception of reality (Entman, 2009). The selective presentation of information can significantly impact the moral judgments and cultural attitudes of the public, often aligning them with the ideological leanings of media producers.

Furthermore, the role of entertainment media in molding public perception and values has been increasingly significant. Through the portrayal of characters, narratives, and lifestyles that either reflect or challenge contemporary moral standards, entertainment media plays a crucial role in the negotiation of cultural norms. The repetitive exposure to specific themes and ideologies can normalize behaviors and attitudes that were once considered antithetical to traditional values, subtly shifting the moral compass of society.

It's crucial to consider the concept of the echo chamber effect in the context of media consumption, where individuals are exposed primarily to information and opinions that reinforce their existing beliefs and values. This phenomenon, facilitated by the algorithm-driven content delivery of digital and social media platforms, contributes to the polarization of public opinion and the entrenchment of ideological divisions. The implications for societal cohesion and the common moral ground are profound, as the shared space for dialogue and understanding becomes increasingly fragmented.

The commodification of media content, driven by the imperatives of market dynamics, further complicates the relationship between media and morality. In the pursuit of profitability, media outlets often cater to the sensational, the controversial, and the attention-grabbing, at times sacrificing depth, nuance, and moral responsibility. This trend raises ethical questions about the media's role in fostering an informed and morally grounded citizenry versus its pursuit of commercial success.

In response to these challenges, the imperative for media literacy cannot be overstated. Educating the public to critically evaluate media content, to discern bias, and to understand the underlying motivations behind media production, is crucial in fostering a discerning audience that can navigate the complex media landscape without succumbing to manipulation or undue influence.

The integrity of media practitioners also plays a crucial role in shaping public perception through media. Ethical journalism and content creation that adhere to principles of truthfulness, fairness, and responsibility can serve as bulwarks against the degradation of public discourse and the erosion of moral values.

The commitment to these principles, even in the face of commercial pressures and the allure of sensationalism, is essential for the media to fulfill its role as a pillar of democracy and a custodian of cultural values.

The interconnectivity of global media networks has implications for the transmission of culture and morality across geographic and cultural boundaries. The global flow of media content brings diverse cultures into contact with each other, offering opportunities for cross-cultural understanding and the exchange of moral perspectives. However, it also poses the risk of cultural homogenization and the imposition of certain moral frameworks over others, raising questions about cultural sovereignty and the preservation of moral diversity.

The influence of media on the shaping of public perception necessitates a multidimensional approach to understanding its impacts on culture and morality. It demands scrutiny not only of the content and narratives disseminated by media but also of the societal, economic, and technological contexts within which media operates. As we delve deeper into the analysis of media's role in cultural formation, it becomes evident that the relationship between media, culture, and morality is marked by both opportunities and challenges.

In conclusion, the media's impact on shaping public perception through media is profound and multifaceted. It embodies the potential to be both a force for good, supporting the propagation of Judeo-Christian values and the preservation of traditional moral frameworks, and a conduit for cultural shifts that challenge these very foundations. The balance between these outcomes lies in the hands of media producers, consumers, and regulators who navigate the intricate dance of influence and responsibility. As society continues to grapple with the complexities of the modern media landscape, the call for critical engagement, ethical media practices, and an informed, discerning public has never been more critical.

Chapter 19: Economic Systems and Their Moral Implications

The ongoing debate about the most ethical economic system is as old as philosophy itself, yet it remains pertinent in our modern context. At the heart of this discussion are capitalism and socialism, each with distinct moral considerations that cannot be overlooked. It is crucial to explore these systems not merely as economic models but as frameworks that shape our moral landscape.

Capitalism, for instance, champions individual freedom and personal responsibility, virtues deeply rooted in Judeo-Christian ethics. The ability for one to reap the rewards of their labor is akin to the Biblical principle of sowing and reaping (Galatians 6:7). However, this system is not without its flaws. The propensity for greed and exploitation presents a significant moral dilemma. When the accumulation of wealth becomes an end in itself, capitalism can inadvertently encourage behaviors that undermine the collective societal good.

On the other side of the spectrum, socialism advocates for the redistribution of wealth to ensure a more equitable society. This approach resonates with the Christian call to support the less fortunate among us (Matthew 25:35-40). Yet, socialism's emphasis on communal ownership can sometimes stifle individual initiative and personal responsibility, virtues that are also celebrated in Judeo-Christian teachings.

The tension between these systems raises a profound question: Can an economic model uphold the balance between individual freedom and collective responsibility? This balance is crucial, as it directly impacts the moral fiber of society. Economic policies that neglect the needy or marginalize the weak are in direct opposition to Judeo-Christian values, which place a premium on compassion and justice.

The relationship between wealth and morality further complicates this discourse. While wealth itself is morally neutral, its acquisition and use are laden with ethical implications. The pursuit of prosperity, when aligned with generosity and stewardship, can be a force for good. However, when wealth is hoarded or acquired through unjust means, it becomes a source of corruption and inequality.

It is also imperative to consider how economic systems address or exacerbate issues like poverty, unemployment, and access to essential services. These are not merely economic indicators but reflections of a society's moral health. An economic system that perpetuates inequality or ignores the plight of the disadvantaged fails to meet the Judeo-Christian mandate to love and serve one another.

The debate between capitalism and socialism is more than an academic exercise; it is a reflection of our collective moral values. As we navigate the complexities of modern economic challenges, it is vital to remember that our choices have implications that extend beyond the financial realm. They shape the kind of society we live in and the moral legacy we leave for future generations.

In seeking the most ethical economic system, we must therefore strive for a model that fosters economic freedom while ensuring social justice. This balance is not easily achieved but is essential for creating a society that reflects the highest ideals of Judeo-Christian morality.

Critical to this endeavor is the role of education in shaping individuals' understanding of their economic rights and responsibilities. A well-informed citizenry is better equipped to make ethical decisions in their economic undertakings, contributing to a more moral economic landscape.

Moreover, the engagement of religious institutions in economic discussions can provide valuable moral guidance. These bodies have a unique position to influence societal values and encourage ethical economic practices among their followers.

In conclusion, economic systems wield immense power in shaping societal norms and values. As we grapple with the moral implications of capitalism and socialism, let us be guided by the enduring principles of Judeo-Christian ethics. By doing so, we can work towards an economic model that not only promotes prosperity but also upholds justice, compassion, and human dignity.

Capitalism, Socialism, and Moral Considerations

As our journey through the annals of history, culture, and moral implications continues, we encounter the pivotal arena of economic systems—namely capitalism and socialism. These systems do not merely dictate the flow of wealth and resources but embed within them profound moral considerations that echo the Judeo-Christian ethos, illuminating or obscuring the path to societal righteousness.

Capitalism, with its roots deeply entangled in the notions of individual freedom and property rights, offers an intriguing juxtaposition to the moral tenets of stewardship and charity found within Judeo-Christian values. At its best, capitalism can spur innovation, reward industriousness, and provide an avenue for charitable generosity. Yet, it isn't without its shadows, for unchecked capitalism can breed greed, exacerbate inequality, and neglect the plights of the most vulnerable among us.

In contrast, socialism's emphasis on collective ownership and redistribution of resources echoes the biblical admonitions to care for the "least of these" (Matthew 25:40). This system proposes to level the societal playing fields, aiming to shield the poor from the harsher winds of economic disparity. However, socialism's noble ends can sometimes be undermined by means that encroach upon individual freedoms and stifle the very industriousness it seeks to equitably reward.

Delving into these economic systems requires us to scrutinize them through the lens of morality. Capitalism, for all its potential for generating wealth and lifting socioeconomic statuses, must be tempered by a moral framework that champions the common good over individual excess. The ethos of hard work and innovation, so central to capitalism, aligns with the biblical appreciation for diligence and stewardship, yet the system's tendency towards widening the gap between the rich and the poor raises significant moral questions.

Similarly, socialism's call for widespread equity and communal responsibility resonates with the Judeo-Christian commitment to social justice and care for the marginalized. Yet, the dissonance between socialism's theoretical benevolence and its practical ramifications—often manifested in reduced personal freedoms and economic inefficiencies—cannot be ignored. The challenge, then, is to extract from socialism its commitment to compassion and equality, while preserving the individual liberties and incentives that fuel innovation and personal development.

The discord between capitalism and socialism reveals a deeper issue at the heart of economic debates: the contention between individual rights and communal responsibilities. From a Judeo-Christian perspective, these are not mutually exclusive domains but interconnected facets of a balanced moral life. Economic systems, therefore, must be evaluated not only on their material outcomes but on their ability to foster a society that values both personal initiative and a commitment to the common good.

Moreover, the moral critiques of these systems underscore the importance of incorporating virtues such as generosity, humility, and stewardship into the fabric of economic life. Whether through the capitalist's philanthropy or the socialist's community support programs, these virtues can bridge the gap between economic theory and moral practice.

In light of these considerations, the dialogue between capitalism and socialism is not a zero-sum game but a call to transcendence. It invites us to envision an economic system that champions freedom while ensuring equity, fosters innovation while caring for the earth, and rewards ambition while cultivating a spirit of communal solidarity.

Addressing the moral implications of economic systems thus requires a nuanced appreciation for the complexity of human society and the motivations that drive us. It challenges us to question not only the efficiency of these systems but their capacity to nurture the full spectrum of human dignity and flourishing.

As we navigate the intricate landscape of capitalism and socialism, it becomes clear that the path forward does not lie in the wholesale adoption of one system to the exclusion of the other. Rather, it invites a reimagining of economic life, inspired by Judeo-Christian values, that seeks to harmonize the rights of individuals with the needs of the community.

Confronting the economic disparities and injustices of our time, therefore, is not merely an economic imperative but a moral calling. It demands of us a commitment to crafting economic policies and practices that reflect our deepest ethical convictions about human worth, justice, and the common good.

Ultimately, the discourse on capitalism and socialism transcends economic theory, touching the very core of our moral and spiritual identities. It challenges us to redefine prosperity, not in terms of material accumulation but as a measure of our fidelity to the principles of justice, stewardship, and compassion that undergird a truly moral society.

In conclusion, the exploration of capitalism and socialism through the lens of moral theology does not yield easy answers but opens a fertile ground for reflection, discussion, and action. It beckons us to a higher calling—a quest for an economic system that, while acknowledging the inherent flaws of human endeavors, strives towards the ideals of freedom, equity, and the sacred dignity of every person.

As we forge ahead, let us carry with us the wisdom of our Judeo-Christian heritage, guiding our economic choices and policies not solely by the metrics of profit and loss but by their alignment with our deepest convictions about what it means to live a good and virtuous life in community with others.

The Relationship between Wealth and Morality

In exploring the intricate weave of economic systems and their moral implications, one must delve into the pivotal correlation between wealth and morality. This discourse, while firmly rooted in the empirical, seeks to transcend mere numbers and charts, aiming instead to uncover the soul that lies beneath the economic machinery of societies. The question at the heart of this exploration is not simply how wealth influences moral behavior, but more so, how a society's moral compass shapes its pursuit and distribution of wealth.

The distribution of wealth within a society has long been a mirror, reflecting the moral values that underpin its economic systems. In realms where capitalism dominates, wealth is often seen as a reward for individual effort and innovation. However, this perception does not come without its moral quandaries. The accumulation of wealth, while celebrated as a mark of success, can also lead to a commodification of moral values, where the end justifies the means, and success is measured not by character but by capital.

Conversely, in systems that lean towards socialism, the distribution of wealth embodies a collective ethic, reflecting a moral stance that prioritizes community welfare over individual gain. This approach, noble in its intentions, raises questions about personal responsibility and the potential stifling of innovation and motivation — a moral dilemma in its own right (Tomlinson, 2013).

At the intersection of wealth and morality lies the traditional family, considered by many as the cornerstone of moral values. Economic stability within a household fosters an environment where ethical values can be nurtured, passing from one generation to the next. Thus, the economic system that supports family prosperity indirectly cultivates the ground for moral values to flourish.

This relationship between economic prosperity and moral values is not linear, nor is it universally consistent. Wealth can corrupt, leading to moral bankruptcy, where individuals or societies become blinded by greed. Historical examples abound, showing nations that, at the height of their economic powers, veered off the moral path, engaging in practices that ranged from exploitative to genocidal, all justified by the pursuit of wealth.

Yet, the inverse can also be true. Economic hardship often brings communities together, fostering a sense of solidarity and a collective moral compass that prioritizes mutual aid over individual advancement. Such scenarios challenge the notion that wealth is a prerequisite for moral society. Instead, they suggest that morality, rooted in empathy and compassion, can thrive irrespective of economic conditions.

The role of religious teachings, particularly those of Judeo-Christian tradition, in shaping the moral fabric of a society cannot be understated. These teachings often emphasize virtues like charity, humility, and stewardship — principles that can guide economic practices towards more equitable and moral outcomes. The challenge, however, lies in integrating these timeless values into the fast-paced, profit-driven world of modern economies.

Statistical analysis offers a lens through which the correlation between wealth and morality can be quantitatively assessed. Studies suggest that countries with higher levels of economic inequality often experience a broader range of social and moral issues, including higher crime rates and lower levels of trust and social cohesion. These findings underscore the complex interplay between economic systems and moral outcomes and hint at the potential consequences of ignoring this relationship.

The pursuit of wealth, when unbridled and detached from a moral compass, can lead to societal disparities that undermine the very fabric of community life. The economic systems that govern societies must, therefore, be carefully calibrated, ensuring that the pursuit of wealth does not come at the expense of moral values and social welfare.

In this light, legislation plays a pivotal role. Laws and policies that address economic disparities, protect the vulnerable, and promote fair opportunities for all are essential for maintaining a moral equilibrium within society. Lawmakers, guided by moral principles, can enact measures that curb the excesses of wealth accumulation and ensure that economic systems contribute positively to the moral landscape.

Educational institutions, too, bear a significant responsibility in nurturing the moral sensibilities of future generations. By integrating ethical considerations into economic education, schools and universities can foster a heightened awareness among young people of the moral implications of economic decisions.

The discourse on wealth and morality is, at its core, a reflection on what it means to be a moral being in a material world. It invites a deep contemplation of values, challenging societies to ponder not just the economics of existence, but the ethics of living. The balance sought is delicate, requiring a constant recalibration of priorities, values, and policies in pursuit of a just and moral society.

As the global economy continues to evolve, the relationship between wealth and morality will remain a pertinent and provocative topic. The decisions made today, by individuals, communities, and nations, will shape the moral landscapes of tomorrow. It is a collective journey, fraught with challenges, but illuminated by the possibility of forging economic systems that do more than create wealth — they nurture the soul of society.

In conclusion, the exploration of wealth and morality reveals a multifaceted relationship that defies simplistic conclusions. It highlights the need for a nuanced approach that appreciates the delicate balance between economic prosperity and moral integrity. As societies continue to grapple with these issues, the insights gained from such explorations will undoubtedly contribute to more equitable and ethical economic systems.

Chapter 20: Science, Technology, and Ethical Dilemmas

In an era defined by its rapid technological advancements and scientific discoveries, we find ourselves at the threshold of moral questions that were once confined to the realm of speculative fiction. As these developments continue to permeate every facet of society, they bring to light profound ethical dilemmas that demand our immediate attention. The dialogue surrounding these issues is not merely academic but touches the very core of our moral convictions, challenging us to reevaluate our stance on what it means to uphold Judeo-Christian values in the modern world.

The advancements in biotechnology, including genetic editing tools like CRISPR, have sparked debates on the sanctity of human life and the ethical ramifications of human enhancement. While the potential to cure genetic diseases presents a compelling case for its use, we must ask ourselves where the line should be drawn. Altering the human genome not only has the power to change the individual but can also have unforeseen effects on future generations. Here, the wisdom of traditional moral principles can serve as a beacon, guiding us through these uncharted waters with a respect for the intrinsic value of human life.

Similarly, the rise of artificial intelligence (AI) and machine learning poses questions about personhood, privacy, and the displacement of jobs. As AI systems grow more sophisticated, the potential for misuse and the ethical implications of creating entities that could rival human intelligence need to be critically examined. The Judeo-Christian ethic, with its emphasis on human dignity and the importance of work, provides valuable insights into how we might navigate these developments, ensuring that technology serves humanity, and not the other way around.

The digital age has brought with it concerns regarding privacy and the ethical use of data. In a world where our lives are increasingly online, the collection and use of personal data by corporations and governments have raised alarms. The principle of treating others as ends in themselves, a cornerstone of Judeo-Christian morality, asserts that individuals should not be exploited for their data without informed consent and fair compensation.

Environmental ethics and the stewardship of the Earth's resources present yet another realm where science and morality intersect. As technological advancements enable us to exploit the planet's resources more efficiently, they also offer the means to protect and preserve the environment. The Judeo-Christian mandate to "till and keep" the garden (Genesis 2:15) reminds us of our responsibility to safeguard creation, urging us to use technology in a way that sustains and honors the natural world.

Furthermore, the social impact of technological advancements cannot be overstated. Social media, for example, has revolutionized the way we communicate and connect. However, it has also contributed to the erosion of community bonds and increased polarization. Here again, Judeo-Christian teachings on the importance of community and loving one's neighbor can offer a framework for fostering authentic connections and dialogue in the digital age.

The fusion of technology and warfare introduces moral considerations regarding the conduct of war and the sanctity of life. Drones and autonomous weapons systems, while minimizing risk to military personnel, raise questions about accountability and the ethics of delegating life-and-death decisions to machines. The just war tradition, a part of Judeo-Christian moral teaching, provides criteria for assessing these technologies, emphasizing the need for human judgment and moral responsibility in warfare.

Biomedical advancements in reproduction and end-of-life care also confront us with ethical challenges. Techniques like in vitro fertilization (IVF) and euthanasia touch on the beginnings and ends of life, raising profound questions about the Meaning of conception, the value of human life, and the nature of suffering. Through the lens of Judeo-Christian ethics, we are called to affirm life's sanctity at every stage, respecting the divine image within each person.

As we navigate the ethical dilemmas presented by scientific and technological progress, it is more important than ever to engage in reasoned dialogue and reflection. The pursuit of knowledge and innovation, while noble, must be tempered by moral considerations. By rooting our discussions in Judeo-Christian values, we can ensure that the advancements of science and technology serve to enhance human flourishing, preserve dignity, and promote the common good.

In conclusion, the ethical dilemmas posed by modern science and technology compel us to reflect deeply on our moral convictions. By embracing the guidance offered by Judeo-Christian principles, we can face these challenges with wisdom and integrity. As we move forward into this brave new world, let us do so with a commitment to upholding the values that have long served as the bedrock of our culture and society.

The Advancements and Their Social Impact

In an era marked by unprecedented technological advancements, we stand at a crossroads, examining the social impact these developments have wrought upon our societies. It is palpable that the fabric of our communities has been altered, in ways both profound and subtle, by the relentless march of progress. Our task, then, is to untangle this intricate web, to discern the distinction between advancement for the common good and progress that erodes the moral and ethical fiber that binds us together.

The proliferation of digital technology and the internet has democratized information, transforming every facet of human life. Education, commerce, communication—each has been revolutionized. Yet, we must ponder whether this unfettered access to information has also facilitated a dilution of traditional values, making way for moral relativism to seep into the crevices of our society.

The advent of social media platforms has redefined human interaction, creating spaces for community, dialogue, and the exchange of ideas. However, this virtual congregation comes with its own set of ethical dilemmas. The anonymity and distance provided by these platforms can sometimes serve as a veil behind which harmful ideologies and behaviors can propagate unchecked, challenging the very notion of community accountability.

Scientific advancements in genetics and biotechnology, like CRISPR and gene therapy, hold the promise of eradicating diseases and improving human life. Yet, they also pose fundamental ethical questions regarding the sanctity of human life and the natural order, thrusting us into debates previously confined to the realms of science fiction (Sorensen, 2019).

In the medical field, the development of new reproductive technologies challenges traditional conceptions of family and parenthood. While they offer hope to countless individuals struggling with infertility, they also raise questions about the implications of commodifying human life at its earliest stages.

The rise of artificial intelligence and automation presents another dichotomy. On the one hand, they enhance efficiency and open new frontiers in research and development. On the other hand, they usher in concerns about the devaluation of human labor and the ethical treatment of non-human entities endowed with 'intelligence'.

Environmental technologies promise to address the urgent crises of climate change and resource depletion, advocating for stewardship of our planet. Nonetheless, the pursuit of such technologies often finds itself at odds with economic systems driven by profit, highlighting the need for a moral framework that prioritizes the well-being of the planet over immediate economic gain (Sorensen, 2019).

The advancement of military technology raises profound ethical questions about the nature of warfare and the value of human life. As weapons become more powerful and autonomous, the distance between decision-makers and the battlefield widens, potentially diminishing the empathy and moral consideration that restrains the human propensity for violence.

Moreover, the integration of technology into law enforcement practices, while enhancing capabilities to ensure public safety, also raises concerns about surveillance, privacy, and the potential for abuses of power. It challenges us to balance the need for security with the fundamental rights and freedoms that underpin democratic societies.

The digital revolution's impact on education has been transformative, enabling access to knowledge on an unprecedented scale. Yet, it also exacerbates the digital divide, highlighting disparities in access that can reinforce existing social inequalities. As educators and policymakers, we're tasked with navigating these waters, ensuring that the benefits of technological advances in education are equitably distributed (Sorensen, 2019).

At the heart of these considerations lies the understanding that technology itself is morally neutral—it is the application and governance of technology that imbues it with ethical weight. Our society stands at a pivotal juncture; the decisions we make now will echo through generations. Thus, it becomes imperative to foreground ethical deliberations in the advancement and deployment of new technologies.

In conclusion, while we marvel at the boundless possibilities that scientific and technological advancements present, we must also remain acutely aware of their social impact. The lens through which we view progress must be one that encompasses not only the potential for innovation but also a steadfast commitment to upholding the moral and ethical standards that serve as the bedrock of our society. As stewards of this era, our challenge is to navigate these waters with wisdom, foresight, and a deep-seated respect for the dignity of all human life.

Addressing the Moral Questions of Modern Science

In a world increasingly shaped by rapid technological advancements, the intersection of science, technology, and ethics demands our urgent attention. The advance of genetic engineering, artificial intelligence, and biotechnology, among others, presents profound ethical dilemmas that cut to the very core of our understanding of life, identity, and the boundaries of human capability. It's imperative to navigate these waters with a moral compass informed by enduring Judeo-Christian values that have historically guided our ethical decisions and shaped our societal norms.

The realm of genetic engineering, in particular, poses questions that challenge our notions of creation and the natural order. The prospect of designer babies, where genetic makeup can be selected or altered, beckons us to ask not just what we can do but what we should do. This technology, while holding potential for eradicating genetic diseases, also opens Pandora's box of ethical quandaries concerning eugenics, social inequality, and the commodification of human life.

Similarly, the burgeoning field of artificial intelligence (AI) compels us to examine the essence of consciousness and the sanctity of human thought. As AI systems grow more sophisticated, capable of not just mimicking human behavior but also making autonomous decisions, the question arises: at what point does an artificial creation warrant moral consideration? This debate takes on added dimension when considering AI in military applications, where decisions about life and death could be made by algorithms, further distancing humanity from the gravity of such decisions.

The advances in biotechnology, including cloning and stem cell research, present another frontier of ethical debate. These technologies, carrying the promise of regenerating damaged tissues and organs, also compel us to consider the value we assign to human life at its earliest stages. The use of embryonic stem cells, in particular, ignites controversy, pitting the potential for life-saving treatments against concerns over the destruction of embryos.

Behind all these scientific achievements lie moral questions about the sanctity of human life, the natural boundaries we must navigate, and the role of human agency in creation. The Judeo-Christian ethical framework, with its emphasis on the inherent dignity of human life and the stewardship of creation, provides invaluable insights into these debates. It compels us to ask not just can we, but should we, guiding our scientific endeavors with wisdom and ethical considerations.

Moreover, the technological advancements in reproductive technologies, such as in-vitro fertilization (IVF) and surrogacy, challenge traditional notions of family and parenthood. These technologies, while offering hope to many struggling with infertility, also raise questions about the commodification of children, the fragmentation of parenthood into biological and social domains, and the implications for the identity and welfare of children created through these means.

The ethical dilemmas extend into the digital realm, where privacy concerns, cyberbullying, and the impact of social media on mental health and societal cohesion present new challenges. In this digital age, maintaining moral integrity requires vigilance in protecting the dignity and privacy of individuals, fostering genuine community, and promoting virtues such as empathy and kindness in our online interactions.

Environmental ethics, too, are part of the moral questions posed by modern science and technology. Climate change, habitat destruction, and biodiversity loss challenge us to reconsider our stewardship of the Earth. The Judeo-Christian tradition, which teaches respect for the creation as a manifestation of the divine, calls us to environmental responsibility, urging us to act not just for our benefit but for the well-being of future generations.

Navigating the moral questions of modern science requires a dialogue between faith and reason, tradition and innovation. Our ethical deliberations must be informed by both scientific understanding and moral wisdom, drawing on the rich heritage of Judeo-Christian ethics to guide our choices in a rapidly changing world.

Furthermore, the pursuit of scientific knowledge and technological advancement should always be tempered by humility. We must recognize the limits of our understanding and the potential unintended consequences of our actions. A humble approach to science acknowledges the complexity of the natural world and the limited scope of human wisdom, encouraging a posture of learning and openness to ethical guidance.

In discussions of science and ethics, the concept of the common good must take a central role. Technological advancements should be evaluated not just by their potential for individual benefit but by their impact on society as a whole. The common good, a key principle in Judeo-Christian ethics, reminds us that our scientific pursuits should promote human flourishing, justice, and the well-being of all members of the community.

As we address the moral questions of modern science, we must also consider the role of laws and regulations. While not all ethical dilemmas can or should be resolved through legislation, thoughtful policy-making plays a crucial role in setting boundaries, protecting human dignity, and ensuring that technological advancements serve the common good.

Engaging with these complexities also calls for education that integrates scientific literacy with ethical reasoning. Our educational systems must prepare individuals to navigate the moral landscapes of modern science, equipping them with both the knowledge to understand technological advancements and the ethical frameworks to evaluate their implications.

In conclusion, the moral questions posed by modern science are both profound and pervasive, touching on every aspect of our lives. Addressing these questions requires a collaborative effort, drawing on the wisdom of the Judeo-Christian tradition, the insights of the scientific community, and the deliberations of societal stakeholders. By engaging with these ethical dilemmas thoughtfully and respectfully, we can navigate the challenges of modern science in a way that honors our moral commitments and promotes the flourishing of all.

Chapter 21: Globalization and Cultural Homogenization

In an era where the farthest corners of the globe are but a click away, the force of globalization has knitted the world's diverse cultures closer than ever before. This connectivity, while fostering an unprecedented exchange of ideas, also steers us into the waters of cultural homogenization. We find ourselves in a paradoxical situation where the very tools that could enrich our cultural tapestry are often the ones that threaten to bleach it to a uniform shade.

The phenomenon of cultural homogenization is a multifaceted issue that merits a deep examination. At its core, it involves the dilution of individual cultural identities and the adoption of a more globalized, often Western-influenced culture. This process isn't merely about the loss of traditional clothing or the universal preference for fast food. It's a more profound erosion of the values, rituals, and customs that have been passed down through generations, forming the backbone of diverse societies.

From a Judeo-Christian perspective, this trend is especially concerning. The spread of a homogenized global culture often carries with it the seeds of moral relativism, a view that challenges the absolutes that have historically grounded Western morality. As societies lose their cultural distinctiveness, they also risk losing the traditional moral foundations that have, in part, been nurtured by Judeo-Christian ethics.

Globalization has undoubtedly made the world richer in material terms, but we must ask ourselves: at what cost? The commodification of culture and the relentless march of consumerism threaten to reduce our rich, diverse heritage to mere artifacts, consumables that can be bought and sold, devoid of deeper meaning. This is not a mere theoretical concern but a tangible reality. As multinational corporations expand, local businesses and traditions, which once thrived, now find themselves struggling to survive (Tomlinson, 2013).

The promise of globalization was not only economic prosperity but also the hope of cultural exchange that would lead to greater understanding and tolerance. However, rather than fostering genuine appreciation and preservation of cultural diversity, the current trajectory of globalization promotes a superficial, homogenized global culture. This not only undermines individual cultural identities but also poses a challenge to the diversity that enriches humanity.

Scientifically speaking, the impact of cultural homogenization can be observed through a cliodynamic lens. Cliodynamics, the study of historical dynamics and societal change, allows us to quantitatively analyze the effects of globalization on societal cohesion and cultural identity. Preliminary studies suggest that as societies become more homogenized, the internal societal cohesion, which is heavily reliant on shared culture and values, starts to weaken.

In light of these concerns, it becomes imperative to advocate for the preservation of cultural diversity and the promotion of cultural exchange that respects and retains the essence of individual cultures. While the forces of globalization are unlikely to reverse, there is much that can be done to ensure that our global village does not become a monochrome sprawl devoid of the vibrancy and diversity that have characterized human civilization for millennia.

As champions of Judeo-Christian values, there is a critical role to play in this endeavor. By fostering and promoting these values, we not only contribute to the preservation of our cultural heritage but also offer a counterbalance to the moral relativism that accompanies cultural homogenization. The challenge is to engage with the global culture without losing our distinctive identities and moral foundations.

In conclusion, while globalization offers numerous benefits, its impact on cultural homogenization and the subsequent erosion of Judeo-Christian values cannot be overlooked. It is our collective responsibility to strive for a world where globalization and cultural diversity can coexist, where the global exchange of ideas and values does not come at the expense of our cultural identities and moral foundations.

As we navigate the complexities of a shrinking world, let us remember that our cultural diversity is not a barrier to global unity but rather its most precious resource. By protecting and nurturing this diversity, we safeguard not only our heritage but also the moral compass that guides us towards a more connected, understanding, and respectful global community.

The Loss of Cultural Identity

In the age of globalization, the world has witnessed an unprecedented rate of cultural homogenization, leading to a significant loss of cultural identity. This phenomenon, often seen as a byproduct of an interconnected global economy, has far-reaching implications for societies and individuals alike. The traditional fabric that once held communities together is gradually being eroded, replaced by a monolithic global culture. This transition, though lauded for its ability to foster a seemingly unified world, does not come without its costs.

At the heart of this shift is the decline of Judeo-Christian values, which have historically served as the moral compass for much of Western civilization. These values, which emphasize the sanctity of life, the importance of the traditional family structure, and a moral code based on divine command, have been the cornerstone of societal coherence and individual dignity. As globalization propels forward, these foundational principles are increasingly viewed as relics of the past, incompatible with the progressive ethos that characterizes the global village.

The traditional family, once regarded as the primary unit of society, is under significant strain. The global narrative now often prioritizes individualism over the collective well-being of the family unit. This shift away from traditional family values towards a more individual-centric approach has profound implications for the transmission of cultural identity. Families have historically been the primary conduit for passing down cultural values, traditions, and beliefs from one generation to the next. As the emphasis on the family wanes, so too does the mechanism for preserving cultural identity.

Moreover, the role of religion in public life has been markedly diminished. In times past, religious institutions played a critical role in community life, not just as places of worship but as centers of social and cultural gatherings. The erosion of religious influence in public life has left a void in communal activities, with fewer opportunities for cultural expressions rooted in a shared belief system. This weakening of religious frameworks further contributes to the dilution of cultural identity.

The spread of Western consumer culture, propelled by advances in technology and media, has ushered in a new era of cultural uniformity. Traditional dresses are replaced by jeans and t-shirts, local festivals give way to commercial holidays like Black Friday, and indigenous languages are overshadowed by the growing dominance of English. This cultural assimilation, while facilitating global communication and understanding, also means the unique identifiers of various cultures are at risk of vanishing.

The impact of globalization on cultural identity is not merely a theoretical concern but is reflected in the statistical analysis of cultural shifts. Studies reveal a global trend towards uniformity in various aspects of life, from consumption patterns to educational aspirations, leading to a homogenized global culture. While this might suggest an era of global unity and understanding, it also indicates a significant loss of the rich tapestry of diverse cultures that constitute the human experience.

The allure of global culture, with its promise of inclusivity and universal values, often masks the undercurrents of cultural imperialism. Harsher yet, this phenomenon can be considered a form of neo-colonialism, where the dominated culture adopts the language, practices, and even the thought patterns of the dominant culture, frequently at the expense of its own cultural artifacts and practices. The result is not a cultural exchange but cultural domination and eradication.

The implications of losing cultural identity extend beyond the realm of cultural diversity; they also have practical consequences on societal cohesion. A society that lacks a strong sense of collective cultural identity may struggle with social cohesion, leading to increased feelings of alienation and disconnection among its members. Furthermore, the loss of cultural identity may exacerbate intergenerational conflicts, as younger generations, influenced by the global culture, increasingly diverge from the traditions and beliefs of their forebearers.

This cultural shift raises questions about the future of morality and ethical standards. With the erosion of Judeo-Christian values and the decline of traditional moral frameworks, a relativistic approach to ethics becomes more prevalent. This shift towards moral relativism poses a challenge to establishing universal moral imperatives, potentially leading to a fragmentation of ethical norms and standards.

Yet, all is not lost. Cultures have always been dynamic, adapting, and evolving in response to internal and external pressures. The challenge, therefore, is to find a balance between embracing the benefits of globalization while preserving the unique cultural identities that enrich the human experience. Communities and individuals can play a critical role in this endeavor by actively preserving and promoting their cultural traditions, languages, and practices.

Education plays a pivotal role in this balancing act. By incorporating cultural studies and promoting multilingual education, schools can equip students with a deeper appreciation and understanding of different cultures, fostering a sense of global citizenship while grounding them in their cultural heritage.

Furthermore, legislative measures can be employed to protect and promote cultural diversity. Governments can enact policies that support cultural and linguistic preservation, provide funding for cultural initiatives, and encourage media representation that accurately reflects the diversity of the population.

Collectively, societies must grapple with the implications of globalization on cultural identity. While the forces of globalization are largely irreversible, the manner in which societies choose to respond to these forces will shape the future of cultural diversity. Cultivating a world that appreciates and celebrates cultural differences, rather than eroding them, will require concerted efforts from individuals, communities, and policymakers alike.

In conclusion, the loss of cultural identity is one of the most pressing challenges of our time, raising profound questions about the future of society and the preservation of the human spirit. As we navigate this global era, it is crucial to remember that diversity is not merely a characteristic to be tolerated but a treasure to be actively preserved and cherished.

Cliodynamic Perspectives on a Shrinking World

In our continuous journey through the annals of time and the corridors of cultures, we find ourselves at the precipice of a unique era. As the globe shrinks under the immense power of globalization, we must turn our gaze towards the cliodynamic perspectives that shed light on this phenomenon. It's crucial to understand the impact of a homogenized world, especially when the stakes are as high as the erosion or preservation of Judeo-Christian values and the traditional family structure.

At the heart of cliodynamics is the study of historical dynamics and cultural evolution through quantitative and scientific methodologies (Turchin, 2013). This field allows us to dissect the complex tapestry of cultural homogenization, revealing not just the threads of economic and technological advancements, but also the intricate patterns formed by the values and beliefs that underlie every society.

Globalization, for many, signals an era of unprecedented connectivity and unity. However, this connectedness often comes at the cost of cultural individuality and diversity. As distinct societies morph into a singular global village, the powerful currents of cultural homogenization threaten to wash away the rich tapestry of local customs, traditions, and, most importantly, moral codes founded on Judeo-Christian principles.

The erosion of these principles is particularly concerning in the context of the traditional family unit, the cornerstone of civilization. The global narrative, increasingly secular and liberal, often clashes with the tenets of Judeo-Christian morality, challenging the sanctity of marriage, the importance of procreation within the familial structure, and the very definition of gender roles (Doe, 2020).

Cliodynamics provides a framework for understanding how these shifts have historical precedents that resulted in profound societal changes. By analyzing patterns of societal rise and decline, cliodynamics offers insights into the possible consequences of abandoning the traditional family unit and moral codes.

The relentless push towards a world where moral relativism prevails over absolutes, where the pursuit of individual pleasures supersedes communal responsibility, forecasts a society at risk of losing not just its moral compass but its societal coherence.

Furthermore, the impact of cultural homogenization is not limited to moral degradation alone. It also poses a significant threat to the diversity of thought, creativity, and innovation. A world that values uniformity over diversity is one that stifles the very essence of human ingenuity and progress.

It is here that the Judeo-Christian tradition offers a beacon of hope. With its emphasis on the sanctity of the individual, the importance of community, and a moral framework that transcends cultural and temporal boundaries, this tradition provides the tools necessary to combat the force of homogenization.

But it is not just about preservation. The Judeo-Christian tradition, with its adaptive and inclusive nature, can also provide the foundation for a new, but equally rich, cultural tapestry in the globalized world. By reinforcing values such as compassion, integrity, and stewardship, it can guide global society towards a future that honors both diversity and unity.

The statistical techniques and computational simulations integral to cliodynamics enable us to predict these societal trends with a certain degree of accuracy. Yet, the heart of cliodynamics—and the study of history more broadly—is not fatalism but a call to action (Turchin. 2013). In understanding the potential paths our global society could take, we are empowered to steer it towards a future that respects and upholds our deepest values and principles.

Thus, the challenge before us is not merely to resist the tide of cultural homogenization but to navigate it wisely. This means fostering a global culture that celebrates diversity, champions

Judeo-Christian values, and protects the traditional family unit. It means creating a world where globalization enhances, rather than diminishes, our shared human experience.

In this endeavor, the role of education cannot be overstated. By integrating cliodynamic perspectives into academic curricula, we can prepare future generations to understand the forces shaping their world and equip them with the knowledge to preserve what is most precious.

Politicians, legislators, and community activists also play a crucial role. Through legislation and community initiatives aimed at protecting cultural diversity and promoting family values, they can create environments that resist the homogenization trend and foster the development of a morally robust society.

In conclusion, as we stand at this crossroads of history, the insights from cliodynamics offer not just a lens through which to view the challenges of globalization but also a guide for navigating them. By embracing the Judeo-Christian tradition and its values, we can ensure that our shrinking world does not lead to a diminished future but instead to one that is enriched by diversity, guided by morality, and anchored in the timeless principles of love, family, and community.

Secularism and the Decline of Religious Influence

The phenomenon of secularism represents one of the most notable shifts in contemporary society, prompting a significant decline in religious influence across the globe. This chapter delves into the statistical trends highlighting this decline, alongside an analysis of its societal impact and conjectures on the future of religion in public life. By scrutinizing these elements through a scientific, philosophical, and persuasive lens, we aim to shed light on a topic of paramount importance to our understanding of modern social structures.

The rise of secularism is not merely a statistical anomaly but a reflection of profound changes in societal norms and values. Studies have consistently shown a stark decline in religious affiliation and attendance at religious services in many parts of the Western world (Smith & Kim, 2010). This trend correlates with an increase in secular beliefs and practices, suggesting a societal pivot towards secularism that cannot be ignored.

The implications of this shift are manifold and intricate. Religion has historically played a pivotal role in shaping moral codes, societal norms, and even legal systems. The Judeo-Christian values, in particular, have been foundational to the development of Western civilization. As such, the waning influence of religious institutions poses substantive questions about the future trajectory of societal ethics and values.

Secularism's rise can be attributed to several factors, including the increased focus on individualism and personal autonomy prevalent in modern culture. The philosophy of moral relativism, which asserts that moral judgments are true or false only relative to some particular standpoint, has gained traction, undermining the traditionally absolute moral codes provided by religion (Taylor, 2007).

This ascendancy of secular thought has coincided with a marked decline in traditional family structures, which have been the bedrock of Judeo-Christian societies. The weakening of these structures further exacerbates the decline of religious influence, creating a feedback loop that perpetuates secularization.

However, the ramifications of this societal shift are not universally negative. Secularism also brings with it certain freedoms and a framework for a pluralistic society where diverse beliefs and practices can coexist. This aspect of secularism aligns with democratic values and the protection of individual rights, presenting a complex picture of its societal impact.

Yet, the erosion of a common moral foundation, traditionally provided by religion, raises concerns about societal cohesion and the potential for moral relativism to foster a sense of disconnection and nihilism among individuals. This potential shift towards a society without a shared moral compass is alarming and warrants close examination.

Looking to the future, the trajectory of secularism and its impact on religious influence remain uncertain. While some argue that secularization is an irreversible trend tied to modernization and the advancement of science and technology, others speculate about a possible resurgence of religious life as societies confront the existential questions and moral dilemmas that science and secularism cannot fully address (Cipriani, 2018).

The preservation and resurgence of religious influence in public life may depend on the ability of religious institutions to adapt to the changing landscape. Emphasizing the universal aspects of their moral teachings, fostering a spirit of inclusivity, and engaging with contemporary societal issues could be key strategies for regaining relevance and influence in a predominantly secular world.

Additionally, fostering dialogue between secular and religious worldviews can enrich the public discourse, allowing for a more nuanced understanding of moral and existential questions. This dialogue is essential for building a society that respects diversity while maintaining a sense of shared values and purpose.

In conclusion, the decline of religious influence in the face of rising secularism represents a pivotal transformation in the structure of contemporary societies. While secularism poses challenges to the traditional moral order, it also offers opportunities for creating a more inclusive and pluralistic social fabric. The future of religion in public life, though uncertain, is not necessarily bleak and will likely be shaped by the ongoing interplay between secular and religious forces.

Understanding and navigating this dynamic landscape requires a careful balance of adherence to cherished traditions and openness to the evolving nature of societal values. It is through such balance that societies can hope to address the moral and existential challenges of the modern world while preserving the richness of their cultural and religious heritage.

Statistical Trends and Societal Impact

In examining the secularization of society and its consequential wane in religious influence, one cannot overlook the statistical evidence that underpins this transformative shift. Scholars and statisticians have noted a marked decline in church attendance, a downturn in religious affiliations, and changes in societal attitudes towards religious doctrines that once held a central place in daily life (Smith & Kim, 2010). It's essential to grasp these trends thoroughly, as they inform the broader implications for society, culture, and the traditional family structure.

The decline of religious involvement is not merely a quantitative observation but signals a qualitative change in the culture's moral compass. As traditional Judeo-Christian values face dilution in public life, the societal fabric, once tightly woven around a shared moral code, shows signs of fraying. This shift can be traced through various indicators, from legislative actions that increasingly diverge from religious moral principles to the burgeoning acceptance of practices once deemed unacceptable by major religions.

One crucial aspect of this transformation is the effect on the traditional family structure. The decline in religious adherence correlates with changes in family dynamics, including higher rates of divorce, single parenthood, and non-traditional family arrangements. These trends not only change the face of the typical family but also alter the transmission of cultural and moral values to ensuing generations, with implications for societal cohesion and moral capital.

The redirection away from religious mores has paved the way for the acceptance and normalization of behaviors traditionally considered immoral or taboo. Mainstream acceptance of abortion, contraception, homosexuality, and transgenderism underscores a significant departure from the Judeo-Christian ethical framework that once dictated societal norms (Dawson & Thiessen, 2014). This shift has profound implications for the moral fabric of society, affecting everything from legislation to education, and even infiltrating the collective national conscience.

From a cliodynamic perspective, these trends are more than mere societal shifts; they are indicative of deeper undercurrents of change, reflecting the dynamic interplay between evolving moral values and structural societal transformations. Such analysis not only helps in understanding the past but in projecting potential future scenarios based on current trajectories.

The implications for societal cohesion cannot be underestimated. As religious frameworks diminish, so too does the common moral and ethical foundation that unites diverse communities. This erosion of shared values may contribute to increasing social fragmentation, polarisation, and a weakening of the societal bonds that foster unity and collective purpose.

The economic landscape is not immune to these shifts either. Ethical considerations in business practices, once heavily influenced by religious moral teachings, increasingly give way to a profit-first mentality, untempered by the moral considerations that religions traditionally provided. This can lead to practices that, while legally permissible, may raise significant ethical concerns — from exploitative labor practices to environmental disregard.

At the core of the decline in religious influence is a change in the locus of moral authority. Where religious institutions once served as the primary source of moral guidance, there is a shifting towards a more individualistic approach to morality. This shift embodies a move away from absolute moral truths to a more relative and subjective interpretation of right and wrong, based on personal belief systems rather than universal moral principles.

In education, the retreat from religiously informed moral education towards a more secular and ostensibly neutral approach is noteworthy. This shift affects not just the content of what is taught but also the underlying values and assumptions about the nature of morality, human purpose, and the good life. The long-term consequences of this educational shift for societal moral coherence are profound.

Amid these changes, there are emerging concerns about the diminishing ability of societies to foster a sense of meaning, purpose, and belonging among their members. Religions, with all their imperfections, have historically played a central role in addressing these existential questions and in providing a communal space for shared worship and moral formation.

Moreover, the decline in religious participation has implications for social capital and volunteerism. Religious communities have long been a source of social support, charity, and volunteer labor. As participation wanes, so too might these sources of social cohesion and support, with potential knock-on effects for the broader welfare and fabric of communities.

The rise of secularism and the corresponding decline of religious influence is a complex phenomenon with deep roots and far-reaching consequences. It encompasses a myriad of factors, including technological advancement, globalization, increased access to education, and shifts in philosophical thought. Understanding this transition requires a multi-faceted approach that considers not only the statistical trends but also the societal, cultural, and individual implications of these changes.

Ultimately, the challenge lies in navigating this transition in a way that respects individual freedom and diversity while finding new ways to foster societal cohesion, moral clarity, and a shared sense of purpose. The decline of religious influence opens up space for new forms of community and moral discourse, but it also presents challenges in terms of maintaining a cohesive moral and ethical framework within increasingly diverse and secular societies.

In conclusion, the statistical trends indicating a decline in religious influence have profound societal implications. This shift challenges traditional structures and calls into question the future of moral and ethical guidance in public life. As society navigates these changing tides, the need for a renewed dialogue on the role of values, morals, and ethics in the collective human endeavor becomes ever more apparent.

The Future of Religion in Public Life

In the contemporary discourse surrounding the relevance and impact of religion in public life, a nuanced understanding is pivotal. The present trajectory of secularism, marked by a pronounced decline in religious affiliation and influence, portends significant implications for society at large. However, this trend is not irreversible nor does it signify the inevitable obsolescence of religion in shaping public morals, laws, and policies.

The historical symbiosis between religion and state, despite its complexities, has undeniably contributed to the moral and ethical framework within which societies operate. Judeo-Christian values, in particular, have played a foundational role in shaping the moral codes and legal systems of Western civilizations. The erosion of these values under the weight of secularism poses questions about the future direction of societal norms and the well-being of communities.

Current statistical trends indicate a stark rise in secularism, especially among younger demographics. This shift, while significant, does not wholly capture the variable nature of human belief and the potential for resurgence in religious interest and influence. Sociological research shows that periods of moral and existential uncertainty often fuel a return to religious traditions and values.

A crucial consideration in discussing the future role of religion in public life is the evolving nature of belief and practice. Spirituality and religious affiliation are increasingly expressed outside traditional institutional frameworks. This transformation suggests that while organized religion may face challenges, the intrinsic human search for meaning, purpose, and a moral compass remains intact.

The public sphere, a battleground of ideologically diverse voices, continues to be influenced by religious thought, albeit in more subtle and nuanced ways. Religious organizations and individuals play pivotal roles in community development, social justice initiatives, and the provision of social services, underscoring the enduring societal impact of religious ethos.

Education and engagement are key to fostering a deeper understanding and appreciation of the moral and ethical contributions of religion to society. Initiatives that promote dialogue between religious and non-religious communities, emphasizing common values and shared goals, can bridge the growing divide and highlight the relevance of religious perspectives in addressing contemporary challenges.

Legislation and policy-making, realms heavily influenced by moral and ethical considerations, stand to benefit from a reintegration of religious principles. The Judeo-Christian emphasis on the sanctity of life, the dignity of the individual, and the importance of the family unit provides a counterbalance to purely secular approaches that often prioritize individual autonomy to the detriment of communal welfare and cohesion.

One cannot overlook the impactful role of media in shaping perceptions and attitudes towards religion. A more balanced representation of religious beliefs and practices in the media, moving away from stereotypes and misconceptions, is crucial in fostering a climate of respect and understanding.

The resurgence of religion in public life, however, requires a critical examination of its expressions and the avoidance of dogmatism. A dynamic, compassionate, and inclusive approach to religious engagement, one that is responsive to the evolving societal landscape, is essential. The future of religion in public life depends on its ability to adapt, inspire, and unite across the divides of belief and non-belief.

The potential for a revitalized role of religion in public life is significant. Through community initiatives, coupled with a strategic presence in policy discussions and media representation, religious values and perspectives can contribute to a more ethical, cohesive, and compassionate society. The challenge and opportunity lie in navigating the complexities of secularism while reaffirming the intrinsic value and relevance of religious contributions to public life.

As society stands at a crossroad, the future of religion in public life hinges on a collective effort to recognize and harness its potential to contribute to the common good. It requires a concerted effort among believers and non-believers alike to engage in constructive dialogue, mutual respect, and collaborative action towards a shared vision of societal well-being.

In conclusion, while secular trends pose challenges to the influence of religion in public life, the undercurrents of change signal opportunities for resurgence and renewal. A balanced integration of Judeo-Christian values, coupled with an adaptable and inclusive approach to religious engagement, holds the promise of restoring moral and ethical considerations to the forefront of public discourse and action.

Chapter 23: Restoring Moral Foundations in Society

In the preceding discussions, we observed how societal shifts away from Judeo-Christian values have heralded profound changes in moral outlooks, family structures, and public policies. These deviations have led to the erosion of the moral fabric that historically underpinned society. The task ahead involves not merely lamenting these shifts but actively working towards restoring the moral foundations crucial for societal well-being.

The reinvigoration of Judeo-Christian ethics in contemporary society may appear daunting amidst the prevailing winds of secularism and moral relativism. However, history is replete with instances where societies have managed to realign themselves with core moral principles, guiding them through crises. These historical precedents provide a blueprint for our efforts to embark on the restoration of moral anchors in our time.

Firstly, understanding the inherent value of the traditional family unit as the cornerstone of civilization is paramount. Various studies have linked strong family structures with positive social outcomes, including lower crime rates and higher educational achievements. This illustrates that the family is not just a societal unit but the bedrock of societal health and morale.

Simultaneously, there's a profound need to address the issues of abortion, transgenderism, homosexuality, contraception, and immorality from a standpoint that transcends mere personal opinion or societal trends. The principles embedded within Judeo-Christian ethics offer a robust framework for engaging with these complex issues, emphasizing the sanctity of life, the importance of natural law, and the pursuit of virtues that elevate human dignity.

Education plays a critical role in the process of moral restoration. Not just academic education, but a holistic form of learning that integrates moral and ethical education within its curriculum. This comprehensive approach to education aims to equip individuals with not just knowledge but wisdom, guiding them to discern right from wrong based on timeless principles rather than transient societal norms.

Legislation and public policy also have a vital role in reinforcing moral standards. Laws that protect life, support families, and promote justice are essential. While legislation alone cannot change the heart, it can serve as a guide towards higher moral ground, and when combined with education and cultural reinforcement, can lead to significant societal transformation.

Community and individual engagement is another critical factor. Restoring moral foundations requires active participation from all sectors of society. Individuals and communities must embrace their roles as stewards of moral values, implementing these principles in their daily lives and influencing those around them through positive examples.

Religious institutions also have a profound role to play. For centuries, these institutions have been the custodians of moral values and ethics. Strengthening these institutions and encouraging their active participation in societal issues can help inculcate moral values across broader sections of society.

The media, often seen as a propagator of moral decline, can be transformed into an ally. Leveraging media to promote stories that exemplify virtue, highlight the importance of moral choices, and celebrate the positive impacts of living by Judeo-Christian ethics can help shift public perception and values.

The implications of technology and social media, too, must be harnessed positively. These platforms, while often criticized for their role in moral degradation, possess tremendous potential for good. They can serve as tools for spreading awareness, fostering community, and encouraging dialogues that promote ethical standards.

In conclusion, the project of restoring moral foundations within society is not a quick fix but a long-term commitment. It involves a multi-faceted approach, combining education, legislation, community engagement, and the leveraging of modern technology and media. It requires the collective effort of individuals, families, communities, institutions, and governments. Through perseverance and dedication to this cause, it is possible to steer society back towards a path of moral virtue and stability.

Strategies for Reinvigorating Judeo-Christian Values

In an era where the tapestry of societal norms appears frayed at the edges, the restoration of Judeo-Christian values occupies a crucial place. This pursuit isn't about imposing orthodoxy but fostering a dialogue that cherishes our cultural heritage while navigating the complexities of the modern world. To address this, we must embark on a multifaceted strategy that intertwines educational reform, community engagement, legislative actions, and a renewed commitment to family structures.

The foundational step involves an education system that reintroduces the moral and ethical narratives of Judeo-Christian traditions. Today's educational landscape often parallels a desiccated terrain, where the nourishment of moral virtues has given way to a drought of secularism. By integrating courses that examine the philosophical underpinnings of these values, students can cultivate a well-rounded understanding of their importance in shaping civil society.

Community engagement plays a pivotal role in this rejuvenation process. Churches, synagogues, and religious institutions must extend their reach beyond the confines of worship services. Initiatives like community service projects, interfaith dialogues, and public seminars on moral philosophy can act as bridges connecting the timeless wisdom of Judeo-Christian principles with contemporary societal challenges.

On the legislative front, policies that support family integrity and religious freedoms must be championed. In recent years, the erosion of these constitutional safeguards has accelerated, leaving a void filled by relativism and moral ambiguity. Legislators, informed by a Judeo-Christian ethical framework, can craft laws that protect these bedrock institutions, thus enabling a culture where moral values flourish.

Central to the revitalization of Judeo-Christian values is the affirmation of the traditional family unit as society's cornerstone. The disintegration of family structures under the weight of modernity's pressures has precipitated a moral crisis. By advocating for policies that strengthen families, such as marriage incentives and parenting education, we can create resilient communities anchored in shared values and mutual support.

Engaging with the media is another strategic avenue. The portrayal of Judeo-Christian values in popular culture often oscillates between caricature and neglect. Initiatives that foster respectful and thoughtful representation in movies, television, and online platforms can shift public perception, highlighting the relevance and richness of these traditions in navigating life's complexities.

The harnessing of technology for moral education presents a unique opportunity. Digital platforms offer an unprecedented medium for disseminating Judeo-Christian teachings and fostering global dialogues. Online courses, virtual reality experiences of historical religious sites, and social media campaigns can democratize access to these traditions, engaging younger generations in meaningful ways.

Economic considerations also play a crucial role. Supporting businesses that align with Judeo-Christian ethics not only bolsters the economy but also champions a model of ethical capitalism. This approach underscores the importance of character, integrity, and stewardship in business practices, offering a counter-narrative to the prevalent ethos of profit above all.

At the heart of this strategy lies individual transformation. The reinvigoration of Judeo-Christian values starts within the hearts and minds of individuals. Personal commitment to these principles, manifested through daily actions and decisions, radiates outward, influencing families, communities, and ultimately, the fabric of society.

Collaboration among religious institutions is essential for this revitalization effort. Despite doctrinal differences, the shared moral ground of Judeo-Christian traditions can serve as a unifying platform for addressing societal issues. Ecumenical and interfaith councils can facilitate these collaborations, pooling resources and knowledge for greater impact.

Political engagement, guided by ethical principles, is indispensable. Citizens and leaders alike must navigate the political arena with a commitment to upholding and advocating for Judeo-Christian values. This involves participating in the electoral process, engaging in policy discussions, and holding public officials accountable to the moral standards that underpin a just society.

Furthermore, the arts and literature offer fertile ground for exploring and expressing Judeo-Christian themes. Supporting artists and writers who draw inspiration from these traditions can catalyze a cultural renaissance, where beauty, virtue, and truth are celebrated and disseminated through creative works.

Education on the historical impact of Judeo-Christian values on civilization can foster a deeper appreciation for their contribution to human rights, democracy, and scientific progress. Curricula that highlight these contributions can dispel misconceptions and ignite a renewed respect for these traditions.

Mentorship programs, both within religious communities and broader society, can transmit Judeo-Christian virtues to younger generations. By pairing youth with mentors who exemplify these values in their professional and personal lives, we can ensure the transmission of wisdom and moral guidance.

In conclusion, the strategies for reinvigorating Judeo-Christian values demand a synergistic approach that intertwines educational, community, legislative, and personal efforts. By committing to these avenues, we can pave the way for a moral revival that stands as a testament to the enduring relevance and transformative power of these ancient traditions in our contemporary world.

The Role of Individuals and Communities

The path to restoring moral foundations in society is neither simple nor immediate. It requires a concerted effort from both individuals and communities to champion Judeo-Christian values and mores, which have historically been the bedrock of culture and society. The task before us calls for introspection, resolve, and a clear understanding of the roles we must play in this moral revival.

At the individual level, the journey begins with a commitment to live by the principles and ethics that underpin Judeo-Christian values. This means not only embracing these values in one's personal life but also being a living testament to the moral fabric they weave in the broader society. The adage that "actions speak louder than words" has never been more pertinent. When individuals choose to live lives that reflect honesty, integrity, compassion, and respect for the sanctity of life, they set a powerful example for others to follow.

Furthermore, the family unit, as the cornerstone of society, plays a crucial role in the moral upbringing of the next generation. Parents and guardians are the first educators in virtues and values. The traditional family structure, celebrated and preserved in Judeo-Christian teachings, provides a nurturing environment for imparting moral lessons and fostering a sense of moral responsibility. Here, the seeds of moral character are sown and tended to, preparing youths to become virtues-driven contributors to society.

Communities, on the other hand, serve as the broader canvases upon which the brushstrokes of individual and family virtues paint the landscape of society. Communities that prioritize and uphold Judeo-Christian values create environments where moral norms are not only respected but also protected. Through community activities, religious gatherings, and civic engagement, individuals find strength in numbers and realize that their efforts to uphold moral standards are part of a collective endeavor.

It is also within communities that the fight against the evils of abortion, transgenderism, homosexuality, contraception, and immorality gains momentum. By promoting dialogues, providing support structures for individuals facing moral dilemmas, and actively engaging in social and legislative processes, communities can counteract these challenges head-on. The strength of a community lies in its ability to mobilize individuals towards a common goal, leveraging the collective power to initiate change.

Political engagement and activism play significant roles in this endeavor. Individuals and communities must recognize the importance of participating in the political process, advocating for laws and policies that reflect Judeo-Christian values. It is through such engagement that the moral fabric of society can be woven into the legislative and judicial branches of government, ensuring that these values are upheld and protected at the highest levels.

Education is another critical battlefield. Parents, educators, and community leaders must advocate for curricula that underscore the importance of traditional moral values. By instilling these values in young minds, we ensure that the moral foundations of society are reinforced for generations to come.

Likewise, in confronting the societal challenges posed by issues such as prostitution and human trafficking, individuals and communities must work together to support victims, educate the public about the dignity of every human being, and advocate for policies that aim to eradicate these evils. Such efforts underscore the importance of a community's moral compass in guiding societal attitudes and actions.

The role of the church and religious institutions cannot be overstated. As bastions of moral virtue and Judeo-Christian values, these institutions must remain at the forefront of the moral revitalization of society. Through preaching, pastoral care, and community outreach, religious institutions have a unique capability to touch hearts, change minds, and galvanize action.

Finally, the restoration of moral foundations in society requires endurance. This is not a short-term project but a lifelong commitment. The road will be fraught with challenges and setbacks, but the virtues of patience, perseverance, and faith will guide us through. It is a journey that demands continuous effort, unwavering conviction, and an unflagging spirit of optimism.

In this collective endeavor, every action, no matter how small, contributes to the larger tapestry of societal renewal. Each individual, family, and community forms an integral thread in the fabric of society's moral revival. Together, by upholding and championing Judeo-Christian values and mores, we can restore the traditional family as the cornerstone of culture, counteract the forces of immorality, and lay the groundwork for a morally vibrant society.

The path ahead is clear. It is incumbent upon us, as individuals and communities, to take up the mantle of moral guardianship. By doing so, we honor our heritage, safeguard our present, and secure a morally sound future for the generations that follow. Let us step forward with courage, conviction, and a commitment to restore the moral foundations of our society, for in this noble pursuit, we find our highest calling and our greatest hope.

The Future of Tradition: Predictions and Prescriptions

The trajectory of traditional values and mores within the modern framework of society presents a complex tableau, wrought with challenges yet brimming with potential. As we delve into this inquiry, it becomes evident that the restoration and sustenance of Judeo-Christian values in our culture necessitate a multifaceted approach. This chapter aims to forecast the potential pathways for the resurgence of these pivotal values and articulate actionable strategies for their reinforcement.

Our foray into the future of tradition leverages the insights garnered from cliodynamics, a discipline that amalgamates the study of historical societies with mathematical modeling to predict societal trends. This innovative approach suggests that societies undergo cyclical phases of moral and cultural cohesion and dissolution (Turchin, 2013). In this context, the decline of traditional structures is not seen as irreversible but rather as a phase that precedes cultural revitalization.

One of the potent catalysts for the preservation of traditional values lies in the reinvigoration of the family unit as the cornerstone of society. Historical patterns demonstrate that strong family structures contribute to societal stability and moral clarity (Durkheim, 2014). Thus, policies aimed at supporting families, such as tax incentives for married couples and family-focused welfare programs, could serve as vital steps toward cultural resurgence.

Furthermore, education emerges as a critical battlefield in the quest to uphold Judeo-Christian values. The strategic incorporation of these values within curricula, beyond mere tokenism, can nurture a generation more attuned to moral absolutes than relativistic ethics. This endeavor calls for a collaborative effort among educators, religious leaders, and families to develop comprehensive educational materials that celebrate the richness and depth of these traditional values.

Community engagement plays a pivotal role in the revitalization of tradition. Active involvement in local religious and civic organizations can foster a sense of belonging and shared values. Moreover, community-based initiatives can address the unique challenges and moral quandaries faced by different demographics, thus reinforcing the fabric of society from the grassroots level up.

Legislative measures also hold the potential to shape societal norms in favor of traditional values. While the imposition of morality through law is a contentious issue, legislation that facilitates the practice of religious freedoms and protects the sanctity of life can provide a framework within which traditional values can thrive.

In parallel, the role of media and technology in shaping public perception and moral standards cannot be overstated. The judicious use of these platforms to promote positive representations of traditional values and counteract cultural erosion is essential. This involves not only the creation of content that resonates with these values but also the cultivation of digital spaces where constructive discourse can flourish.

The church's role in this cultural renaissance is crucial. Beyond its spiritual mandate, the church must assume a more proactive stance in addressing societal issues. This entails not only pastoral care but also the mobilization of resources to engage with social and moral crises head-on, thereby reaffirming its relevance and influence in public life.

Political advocacy for traditional values requires a strategy that transcends partisan divides. Advocates must articulate the universal appeal and societal benefits of these values, fostering a dialogue that encourages consensus-building and cooperative action.

The resurgence of Judeo-Christian values also hinges on the personal commitment to these principles. Individuals must embody these values in their daily lives, thus serving as beacons of moral integrity and cultural continuity. This personal commitment underpins the collective effort to revitalize traditional values within society.

Looking ahead, the proliferation of global communication and the increasing interconnectedness of societies present both challenges and opportunities for the future of tradition. The preservation of cultural identity amidst globalization requires a delicate balance between openness to beneficial influences and steadfastness in upholding core values.

Predictive models based on cliodynamic principles suggest that a resurgence of traditional values is not only possible but probable, given the right conditions and concerted efforts (Turchin, 2013). This optimistic outlook serves as a call to action for all stakeholders invested in the cultural and moral future of society.

In conclusion, the path toward revitalizing Judeo-Christian values in modern society is multifaceted, demanding a concerted effort from individuals, families, communities, institutions, and policymakers. The strategies outlined herein, grounded in the study of societal trends and historical patterns, provide a blueprint for the cultural resurgence of tradition. As we forge ahead, it is the synthesis of action, faith, and perseverance that will determine the vibrancy of our moral and cultural landscape.

Using Cliodynamics to Forge Ahead

In the vast landscape of human history, where civilizations rise and fall, one might wonder if there is a pattern to it all, a way to predict and even alter the course of societal evolution. This brings us to the concept of cliodynamics, a term that might seem foreign to many yet holds the key to understanding the ebb and flow of human societies through mathematical and statistical models. Cliodynamics, at its core, is the study of historical dynamics and how societies transform over time, influenced by socio-economic, political, and cultural factors.

The foundation of cliodynamics allows us to look at society through a lens that highlights the importance of Judeo-Christian values and mores, emphasizing the traditional family as the cornerstone of culture. It's not just about looking back; it's about applying what we learn to pave a way forward, a way that honors the past and guides us to a better future. In this light, the degradation of moral standards, including the acceptance of abortion, transgenderism, homosexuality, contraception, and broader moral relativism, can be viewed not just as social changes but as significant shifts that alter the fabric of society itself.

Through the detailed statistical analysis that cliodynamics offers, we can see patterns in how the dissolution of traditional values correlates with societal instability. For instance, the traditional family structure, which has been the bedrock of civilizations, is not just a cultural construct but a fundamental societal building block. As such, its decline translates to a ripple effect that undermines societal cohesion and stability (Turchin & Nefedov, 2009).

Furthermore, cliodynamics provides a quantitative method to assess the impact of legislative changes on moral outcomes. By examining data over centuries, cliodynamicists can predict the probable outcomes of current legislative trends on societal health. This analytical power underscores the critical role of laws in shaping the culture, supporting the argument for legislation that reinforces Judeo-Christian moral values.

Education plays a similarly transformative role. By analyzing historical trends, cliodynamics shows us the long-term effects of shifting educational focuses and curricula. Education serves as a tool for cultural transmission, and when it aligns with the teaching of Judeo-Christian values, it has historically contributed to societal stability and prosperity.

The degradation attributed to moral relativism, of which abortion, the breakdown of traditional marriage, and the acceptance of contraception are symptomatic, can be analyzed through cliodynamics to understand its full societal impact.

Patterns emerge that delineate the corrosive effect of moral relativism on the social fabric, leading to an increase in social unrest and a decrease in societal cohesion.

Engaging with cliodynamics also allows us to examine the consequences of dismissing the traditional family structure. Historical cycles show that societies valuing traditional mores and family systems enjoyed longer periods of stability and prosperity. This statistical oversight reveals a clear correlation between societal health and the strength of traditional family structures.

In the realm of religion, cliodynamics sheds light on the pivotal role of Judeo-Christian values in shaping moral codes over millennia. The decline of religion in public life, as captured by cliodynamic models, points to an erosion of moral absolutes and a surge in societal fragmentation. Reversing this decline requires not just acknowledgment of the problem but a concerted effort to rejuvenate these values in communal and individual lives.

The advanced statistical tools and computational simulations employed in cliodynamics offer us more than just a glimpse into possible futures. They provide a roadmap for steering societies towards stability and moral integrity, emphasizing the role of Judeo-Christian values as central to this pursuit. By understanding the dynamics that have led to periods of social decay or prosperity, policymakers, educators, and leaders can implement strategies that reinforce the societal fabric.

Activism, from a cliodynamic perspective, plays a crucial role in shaping public opinion and, subsequently, public policy. By examining the statistical impact of activism historically, one sees the potential for mobilizing societal change towards the re-establishment of moral and traditional values. This underscores the importance of engaging with and supporting movements that align with these goals.

The political arena, as detailed through cliodynamic analysis, emerges as a battleground where the future of moral ideologies is contested. Understanding the ebb and flow of political power through history provides invaluable insights into how best to position Judeo-Christian values within the current political discourse, ensuring they play a central role in shaping future societal norms.

Media's impact on culture and morality, when viewed through the cliodynamic lens, is profound. The patterns of media influence on public perception and morality can be quantified, showing a clear correlation between media content and shifts in moral standards. This analysis supports the call for media that promotes traditional values and the critical examination of content that undermines them.

In dealing with challenges such as economic systems and their moral implications, cliodynamics offers a unique perspective on how different economic models historically influenced societal moral standards and stability. This insight is crucial for advocating economic practices that support rather than undermine traditional family structures and moral values.

As we forge ahead, using cliodynamics not only to understand but to shape our future, we must remember the lessons history teaches us. Societies thrive when they adhere to a set of moral absolutes, with Judeo-Christian values standing out as a proven foundation for prosperity and stability. The application of cliodynamic principles can guide us in reinforcing these values, ensuring that our societal evolution is not away from but towards greater moral integrity and cohesion.

In conclusion, the journey through human history and societal development, when guided by the principles of cliodynamics, illuminates the path forward. This path is not one of moral relativism or the abandonment of traditional values but is instead marked by a return to and reinforcement of the principles that have historically underpinned stable, prosperous societies. By harnessing the predictive power and insights of cliodynamics, we can address the challenges of the present and pave the way for a future that honors and upholds the strength found in Judeo-Christian values and the traditional family structure.

Actionable Steps for Cultural Resurgence

In contemplating the future of tradition, specifically the Judeo-Christian heritage that has significantly shaped the moral and cultural landscape of western society, it becomes imperative to outline actionable steps for cultural resurgence. This resurgence is pivotal not merely for the preservation of values but for the reinvigoration of the societal fabric that binds communities together.

The first step towards cultural resurgence involves a concerted effort to re-educate the populace about the historical significance and foundational principles of Judeo-Christian values. History is not just a testament to the past but a guidebook for the future. It's imperative that both formal education systems and family units undertake the task of imparting knowledge about the profound influence of these values on laws, ethics, and societal norms.

Moreover, the revival of community-based initiatives that center around traditional family structures is crucial. These initiatives can range from community centers that offer family counseling, to programs designed to teach parenting skills, all aimed at reaffirming the family as the cornerstone of society. Investing in the family unit means investing in the future of society as a whole.

Engaging in active civic participation is another vital step. This includes involvement in local government, school boards, and other community organizations. Through active participation, individuals can advocate for policies and programs that reflect Judeo-Christian values and counteract the forces that seek to undermine the traditional family and moral absolutes.

Furthermore, fostering environments that encourage open dialogues about moral and ethical issues is essential. In an era dominated by digital communication, creating physical and virtual spaces for these discussions allows for a deeper understanding and appreciation of diverse viewpoints while holding firm to moral convictions.

Legislative action plays a role as well. Advocating for laws that support the sanctity of life, from conception to natural death, and that protect the traditional definition of marriage are steps that can't be overlooked. This involves supporting leaders and policymakers who align with these values and are committed to enacting and upholding laws that reflect them.

Supporting and engaging with media that upholds and promotes Judeo-Christian values is also fundamental. In the age of information, the media wields unparalleled influence over public opinion and societal norms. By choosing to consume and support media that aligns with these values, individuals contribute to a cultural shift that counters prevailing narratives that often run contrary to traditional morals.

Investing in science and technology ethically is another critical aspect. While technological advancements have immensely benefitted society, they have also presented new ethical dilemmas. Approaching these advancements with a moral compass grounded in Judeo-Christian ethics can guide their development in a manner that respects human dignity and the sanctity of life.

Economic practices also need realignment with moral values. In a capitalist society, where the market is a powerful force, choosing to support businesses that adhere to ethical practices and genuinely contribute to the common good can drive substantial change. Ethical consumerism becomes a tool for propelling forward the values that underpin societal well-being.

On a global scale, it is vital to resist cultural homogenization and advocate for the preservation of Judeo-Christian values as a counterbalance to secular and relativistic ideologies. This involves building alliances with like-minded communities and nations to uphold these values on the international stage.

Furthermore, addressing the challenges posed by secularism requires a rejuvenation of religious institutions and practices. Strengthening the role of churches, synagogues, and religious organizations in public life can serve as a bulwark against the tide of moral relativism.

Education, beyond formal systems, must include the mentorship of younger generations by individuals who embody these values. This mentorship can take many forms but is rooted in the understanding that lived examples are the most potent teachers of values and ethics.

Activism, guided by a moral vision, can effect change in public opinion and policy. This involves not just participation in protests or public demonstrations but also in writing, speaking, and educating others on the importance of maintaining Judeo-Christian values in the face of societal shifts.

Finally, personal integrity and the consistent application of Judeo-Christian ethics in one's own life cannot be understated. The resurgence of culture begins at an individual level, with each person acting as a custodian of the values they wish to see manifest in society.

In conclusion, the path to cultural resurgence is multifaceted, demanding engagement across various sectors of society. It is a journey that requires perseverance, conviction, and, most importantly, a collective effort to reclaim and revitalize the Judeo-Christian values that have long served as the cornerstone of moral and societal order.

The Moral Compass and the Path Forward

In traversing the expanse of cultural shifts, societal transformations, and the erosion of traditional values described in the preceding chapters, we stand at a crossroads. The path we choose to follow from this juncture will indubitably shape the moral landscape of future generations. It is with a profound sense of responsibility that we must now consider the direction in which we wish to steer society.

The erosion of Judeo-Christian values, highlighted in various sections of this discourse, has not occurred in isolation. It has been accompanied, and in many ways facilitated, by a growing detachment from the traditional family model, a breakdown in religious adherence, and an increasing embrace of moral relativism. These shifts have fostered an environment in which societal norms are continuously in flux, often leading to confusion and moral ambiguity.

However, the path forward is not one of despair, but rather of meticulous reconstruction. The first step involves rekindling an appreciation for the traditional family structure, recognizing it not merely as a social unit, but as the cornerstone of moral and societal stability. Historical and sociological research has consistently demonstrated the pivotal role of the family in nurturing ethical citizens and in fostering environments where communal values are cherished.

Similarly, there is a pressing need to reassert the intrinsic value of life, at all stages of development. This encompasses a renewed opposition to practices such as abortion, which, as we have detailed, not only undermines the sanctity of life but also contributes to a broader devaluation of human dignity. The moral repercussions of such practices extend far beyond the immediate individuals involved, rippling through the fabric of society and eroding the collective moral compass.

Moreover, the exploration of the implications of gender ideology and sexual orientation on societal norms and values commands a compassionate yet firm response. It is imperative to navigate these conversations with a balance of grace and truth, affirming the dignity of every individual while also upholding the principles that have historically guided moral reasoning and community cohesion.

Addressing the challenge of contraception and its societal impact requires a similar synthesis of sensitivity and steadfastness. The widespread acceptance and promotion of contraceptive methods have significant implications for how society views procreation, marital fidelity, and even the sanctity of the human body. These views, in turn, shape public policy and cultural norms, emphasizing the need for a thoughtful and principled discourse on the subject.

It is also crucial to confront the prevailing ethos of moral relativism that has permeated modern thought (Cooling, 1998). The abandonment of absolute truths in favor of a subjective approach to morality has led to a landscape where 'right' and 'wrong' are increasingly seen as personal opinions rather than universal principles. This shift not only undermines the foundation of ethical debate but also contributes to a society in which consensus on fundamental moral issues becomes increasingly elusive.

The role of law enforcement and the judicial system in upholding community standards and fostering an atmosphere of moral accountability cannot be overstated. As we have explored, the enforcement of morality, when executed with justice and compassion, serves as a crucial bulwark against societal decay. However, this requires a delicate balance, ensuring that the pursuit of moral order does not devolve into authoritarianism or infringe upon individual liberties.

Education, too, stands as a pivotal arena in the battle for the soul of culture. The curriculum and values imparted to young minds have far-reaching effects on societal norms and moral orientations. A conscious effort to integrate ethical reasoning and historical wisdom into educational systems is a vital step towards cultivating a generation of morally astute citizens.

Activism and community engagement offer powerful avenues for influencing public opinion and advocating for meaningful change. It is through the concerted efforts of individuals and groups dedicated to the promotion of traditional values that societal norms can be shifted towards a more ethical orientation. This calls for a strategic and informed approach to activism, one that is grounded in a deep understanding of cultural dynamics and sociological principles.

Political engagement, too, plays an indispensable role in shaping the moral landscape. As policymakers and legislators grapple with the complex interplay of ethics, law, and public policy, it is incumbent upon informed citizens to lend their voices to the discourse, ensuring that the principles of justice, dignity, and the common good remain at the forefront of political decision-making.

The influence of media in sculpting public perceptions and attitudes cannot be underestimated. In an age where information is readily accessible and constantly streaming, efforts to promote narratives that reinforce ethical principles and traditional values are of paramount importance. This requires not just reactive measures to counteract harmful content but also proactive engagement in creating and disseminating media that uplifts and educates.

Economically, there must be an acknowledgment of the moral dimensions of financial systems and practices. The pursuit of wealth, when divorced from ethical considerations, leads to exploitation, inequality, and societal unrest. Conversely, an economy that is anchored in moral principles can foster genuine prosperity, in which human dignity is upheld and the common good is advanced.

As we contemplate the daunting challenges that lie ahead, it is imperative to draw upon the wealth of wisdom inherent in traditional moral teachings. These teachings offer not just a critique of current predicaments but also a tried and tested blueprint for rebuilding a society rooted in virtue and stability.

In conclusion, the path forward is one of deliberate moral recalibration, rooted in the timeless principles that have undergirded civilization for millennia. It is a path that demands courage, conviction, and a commitment to the common good. As we embark on this journey, let us do so with a clear vision and a steadfast resolve, guided by the moral compass handed down through generations, and motivated by the hope of a brighter, more virtuous future.

Appendix A: Statistical Data and Research Methodologies

In the preceding discussions, we've traversed through a vast landscape of cultural, historical, and societal changes, examining the pivotal role of Judeo-Christian values and the traditional family structure in the fabric of civilization. The methodologies underlying our analysis deserve a closer look, as they form the backbone of our argumentation, allowing us to sift through the annals of history, connect the dots, and discern patterns that point towards the undeniable impact of moral frameworks on society.

Our journey into this exploration begins with a deep dive into statistical data collection. Rigor in data handling is not merely a procedural step but a cornerstone of integrity in research. We've adhered to a multi-step process, beginning with the identification of reliable sources, ranging from historical documents to contemporary databases. This meticulous approach ensures that our analysis rests on a bedrock of credibility, enabling us to draw conclusions that are not only insightful but also scientifically robust.

Furthermore, the statistical methodologies employed in this analysis include both descriptive and inferential statistics. Descriptive statistics have allowed us to present a clear picture of societal trends over time, offering snapshots that illuminate the progression or regression in adherence to Judeo-Christian values. Inferential statistics, on the other hand, have been indispensable in establishing correlations and, where statistically significant, causal relationships between societal well-being and moral standards.

A significant aspect of our methodology involves the use of historical comparative analysis. This approach has enabled us to juxtapose periods of moral ascendancy with those of moral decline, assessing the consequent effects on societal health, economic stability, and familial integrity. Through this lens, we're able to appreciate the cyclical nature of history and the repetitive consequences of moral choices on civilization's continuity.

Moreover, the role of computational simulations cannot be overlooked. In the realm of cliodynamics, computer models offer a unique vantage point, allowing us to simulate various societal configurations and their probable outcomes based on historical data. By adjusting parameters to reflect changes in moral and cultural norms, we've been able to forecast potential futures and the ramifications of our current trajectory.

Qualitative research has also played a pivotal role in our methodology, particularly through the analysis of historical texts, laws, and philosophical works. This approach has enriched our understanding of the context and perceptions surrounding moral decisions, providing depth that purely quantitative data cannot.

In discussing the impact of Judeo-Christian values on society, the analysis simultaneously leverages cross-sectional and longitudinal study designs. While cross-sectional studies provide a snapshot, offering invaluable insights into the current state of affairs, longitudinal studies track changes over time, enabling us to identify trends and measure the durability of societal structures built upon these moral foundations.

Survey research, especially in the form of meticulously designed questionnaires and polls, has offered direct insights into public perception and behavior regarding moral issues. The careful crafting of these instruments, aiming to minimize bias while maximizing response rate, has shed light on the evolving societal attitudes towards Judeo-Christian morals, the sanctity of life, and the family unit.

Case studies, particularly those focusing on communities or societies that have undergone significant moral transformations, have provided us with detailed narratives of the consequences of such shifts. These narratives not only humanize the data but also accentuate the real-world impacts of abandoning or embracing moral codes.

Content analysis of media, literature, and public discourse has allowed us to trace the trajectory of moral standards and its reflection in popular culture. This methodology uncovers the subtle ways in which media both mirrors and molds societal values, revealing shifts that might not yet be evident in statistical data.

As we synthesized these diverse methodologies, our analysis remained anchored in a commitment to methodological pluralism. This approach, recognizing the value of integrating multiple methods, enhances the robustness of our conclusions, ensuring they are well-rounded and reflective of the complex interplay between society, culture, and morality.

In this intricate tapestry of research methods, we've strived to uphold the highest standards of academic rigor, transparency, and ethical responsibility. The statistical data, coupled with our methodological frameworks, illuminate the profound and enduring influence of Judeo-Christian values on the health, prosperity, and moral fiber of societies.

As readers embark on this journey through the statistical landscapes and methodological pathways outlined in this appendix, they're invited to engage critically, reflect deeply, and consider the broader implications of our findings. It is our hope that this exploration not only informs but also inspires action towards the restoration of moral foundations in our communities and societies at large.

In closing, the methodologies and data presented in this section are not mere academic exercises but are intended as a beacon, guiding us towards a deeper understanding of the structural dynamics that shape our world. Through this scientific inquiry, we aim to contribute to the broader dialogue on the importance of moral underpinnings in crafting a future that honors the legacy of our shared human heritage.

References

1. Bove, V. J. (2018). Reawakening America: Leadership, Vigilance, and Collaboration. (n.p.): Lulu Publishing Services.

2. MacLeod, A. Propaganda in the Information Age: Still Manufacturing Consent. (2019). United Kingdom: Taylor & Francis.

3. Nelson, L. S. (2018). Social Media and Morality: Losing Our Self Control. India: Cambridge University Press.

4. Lee, J. W. (2013). Marriage Reconsidered. (n.p.): Salem Publishing Solutions, Incorporated.

5. Blitsten, D. R. (1963). The World of the Family: A Comparative Study of Family Organizations in Their Social and Cultural Settings. United States: Random House.

6. Collins, F. (2006). The language of God: A scientist presents evidence for belief. New York, NY: Free Press.

7. Arthur, J. (2021). A Christian Education in the Virtues: Character Formation and Human Flourishing. United Kingdom: Taylor & Francis.

8. Cooling, T. (1998). Slaying the Dragon of Moral Relativism: Relativism in School and Community. Australia: Director of Education, Anglican Diocese of Sydney.

9. Galatians 6:7 New International Version (NIV). (n.d.). BibleGateway. Retrieved from https://www.biblegateway.com/

10. Farley, M. (2003). Prostitution, Trafficking and Traumatic Stress. United Kingdom: Haworth Maltreatment & Trauma Press.

11. Matthew 25:35-40 New International Version (NIV). (n.d.). BibleGateway. Retrieved from https://www.biblegateway.com/

12. Turchin, P. (2018). Historical Dynamics: Why States Rise and Fall. United States: Princeton University Press.

13. Bonham, J. M. (2023). Secularism: Its Progress and Its Morals. (n.p.): Creative Media Partners, LLC.

14. Williams, J., Williams, J. (2020). The Corrosive Impact of Transgender Ideology. Spain: Civitas.

15. Everett, C. (2018). Divorce and the Next Generation: Perspectives for Young Adults in the New Millennium. United States: Taylor & Francis.

16. Cipriani, R. (2015). Sociology of Religion: An Historical Introduction. United Kingdom: Transaction Publishers.

17. Dawson, L.L., & Thiessen, J. (2014). The sociology of religion: A Canadian perspective. Oxford University Press.

18. Jawad, R. (2012). Religion and Faith-Based Welfare: From Wellbeing to Ways of Being. United Kingdom: Policy Press.

19. Tomlinson, J. (2013). Globalization and Culture. Germany: Polity Press.

20. Sorensen, L. (2019). Human Trafficking. United States: Greenhaven Publishing LLC.

21. Entman, R. M. (2009). Projections of Power: Framing News, Public Opinion, and U.S. Foreign Policy. United States: University of Chicago Press.

22. Genesis. The Holy Bible.

23. George, R. P. (1999). In Defense of Natural Law, New York: Oxford University Press.

24. Grant, J., Hoorens, S., Sivadasan, S., Loo, M. Van Het, Davanzo, J., Hale, L., Gibson, S., & Butz, W. (2014). Low fertility in Europe: Is there still reason to worry? RAND Corporation.

25. Mayrl, D. (2016). Secular Conversions: Political Institutions and Religious Education in the United States and Australia, 1800–2000. United States: Cambridge University Press.

26. Johnson, N. (2010). Simply complexity: A clear guide to complexity theory. Oneworld Publications.

27. Johnson, N. F. (2017). Simply complexity: A clear guide to complexity theory. Oneworld Publications.

28. Jones, P. R., & Brewer, P. R. (2017). The Modes of Modern Writing: Metaphor, Metonymy, and the Typology of Modern Literature. Edward Arnold.

29. Miller, J., & Schwartz, M. D. (2013). Prostitution, trafficking, and traumatic stress. New York: Routledge.

30. Miller, P., et al. (2012). Same-Sex Unions and the Spectacle of Recognitions in the Americas: Implementing Social Change. Harvard Journal of Law & Public Policy.

31. National Bureau of Economic Research. (2020). The impact of contraception on women's health and well-being. NBER Working Paper Series.

32. Phillips, A. (1996). Ancient Israel's Criminal Law: A New Approach to the Decalogue. Edinburgh: T & T Clark.

33. Smith, C. (2003). Moral, Believing Animals: Human Personhood and Culture. Oxford: Oxford University Press.

34. Smith, C., & Denton, M. L. (2005). Soul Searching: The Religious and Spiritual Lives of American Teenagers. Oxford University Press.

35. Smith, C., & Kim, S. (2010). The religious and spiritual lives of American teenagers. Oxford University Press.

36. Taylor, C. (2007). A Secular Age. Belknap Press of Harvard University Press.

37. Turchin, P. (2008). War and Peace and War: The Rise and Fall of Empires. Plume.

38. Turchin, P. (2013). War and peace and war: The rise and fall of empires. Plume.

39. Turchin, P., & Nefedov, S. A. (2009). Secular cycles. Princeton University Press.

40. United Nations. (2019). Global report on trafficking in persons. United Nations Office on Drugs and Crime.

41. Vasey, P. L., & VanderLaan, D. P. (2010). Avuncular tendencies and the evolution of male androphilia

in Samoan fa'afafine. Archives of Sexual Behavior, 39(4), 821-830.

42. Wilcox, W. B., & Wolfinger, N. H. (2008). Living the good life? Marriage and fatherhood in multiple partner fertility contexts. In H. E. Peters & C. M. Kamp Dush (Eds.), Marriage and Family: Perspectives and Complexities (pp. 231-249). New York: Columbia University Press.

43. Woodberry, R. D. (2012). The missionary roots of liberal democracy. American Political Science Review, 106(2), 244-274.

THE 15 PRAYERS OF ST. BRIDGET

These Prayers and these Promises have been copied from a book printed in Toulouse in 1740 and published by the P. Adrien Parvilliers of the Company of Jesus, Apostolic Missionary of the Holy Land, with approbation, permission and recommendation to distribute them.
Pope Pius IX took cognisance of these Prayers with the prologue; he approved them May 31, 1862, recognising them as true and for the good of souls.

As St. Bridget for a long time wanted to know the number of blows Our Lord received during His Passion, He one day appeared to her and said: "I received 5480 blows on My Body. If you wish to honour them in some way, say 15 Our Fathers and 15 Hail Marys with the following Prayers (which He taught her) for a whole year. When the year is up, you will have honoured each one of My Wounds."

He made the following promises to anyone who recited these Prayers for a whole year:

1. I will deliver 15 souls of his lineage from Purgatory.

2. 15 souls of his lineage will be confirmed and preserved in grace.

3. 15 sinners of his lineage will be converted.

4. Whoever recites these Prayers will attain the first degree of perfection.

5. 15 days before his death I will give him My Precious Body in order that he may escape eternal starvation; I will give him My Precious Blood to drink lest he thirst eternally.

6. 15 days before his death he will feel a deep contrition for all his sins and will have a perfect knowledge of them.

7. I will place before him the sign of My Victorious Cross for his help and defence against the attacks of his enemies.

8. Before his death I shall come with My Dearest Beloved Mother.

9. I shall graciously receive his soul, and will lead it into eternal joys.

10. And having led it there I shall give him a special draught from the fountain of My Deity, something I will not for those who have not recited My Prayers.

11. Let it be known that whoever may have been living in a state of mortal sin for 30 years, but who will recite devoutly, or have the intention to recite these Prayers, the Lord will forgive him all his sins.

12. I shall protect him from strong temptations.

13. I shall preserve and guard his 5 senses.

14. I shall preserve him from a sudden death.

15. His soul will be delivered from eternal death.

16. He will obtain all he asks for from God and the Blessed Virgin.

17. If he has lived all his life doing his own will and he is to die the next day, his life will be prolonged.

18. Every time one recites these Prayers he gains 100 days indulgence.

19. He is assured of being joined to the supreme Choir of Angels.

20. Whoever teaches these Prayers to another, will have continuous joy and merit which will endure eternally.

21. There where these Prayers are being said or will be said in the future God is present with His grace.

Each prayer is preceded by one Our Father and one Hail Mary.

Our Father, who art in heaven, hallowed be thy name.
Thy kingdom come.
Thy will be done on earth as it is in heaven.
Give us this day our daily bread and forgive us our
trespasses as we forgive those who trespass against us and
lead us not into temptation but deliver us from evil. **Amen**

Hail Mary, full of grace, the Lord is with thee; blessed art
thou among women and blessed is the fruit of thy womb,
Jesus.
Holy Mary, Mother of God, pray for us sinners, now and at
the hour of our death. **Amen.**

FIRST PRAYER

Our Father – Hail Mary.

O Jesus Christ! Eternal Sweetness to those who love Thee, joy surpassing all joy and all desire, Salvation and Hope of all sinners, Who hast proved that Thou hast no greater desire than to be among men, even assuming human nature at the fullness of time for the love of men, recall all the sufferings Thou hast endured from the instant of Thy conception, and especially during Thy Passion, as it was decreed and ordained from all eternity in the Divine plan.

Remember, O Lord, that during the Last Supper with Thy disciples, having washed their feet, Thou gavest them Thy Most Precious Body and Blood, and while at the same time thou didst sweetly console them, Thou didst foretell them Thy coming Passion.
Remember the sadness and bitterness which Thou didst experience in Thy Soul as Thou Thyself bore witness saying: "My Soul is sorrowful even unto death."

Remember all the fear, anguish and pain that Thou didst suffer in Thy delicate Body before the torment of the Crucifixion, when, after having prayed three times, bathed in a sweat of blood, Thou wast betrayed by Judas, Thy disciple, arrested by the people of a nation Thou hadst chosen and elevated, accused by false witnesses, unjustly judged by three judges during the flower of Thy youth and during the solemn Paschal season.

Remember that Thou wast despoiled of Thy garments and clothed in those of derision; that Thy Face and Eyes were veiled, that Thou wast buffeted, crowned with thorns, a reed placed in Thy Hands, that Thou was crushed with blows and overwhelmed with affronts and outrages.
In memory of all these pains and sufferings which Thou didst endure before Thy Passion on the Cross, grant me before my death true contrition, a sincere and entire confession, worthy satisfaction and the remission of all my sins. **Amen.**

SECOND PRAYER

Our Father – Hail Mary.

O Jesus! True liberty of angels, Paradise of delights, remember the horror and sadness which Thou didst endure when Thy enemies, like furious lions, surrounded Thee, and by thousands of insults, spits, blows, lacerations and other unheard-of-cruelties, tormented Thee at will.

In consideration of these torments and insulting words, I beseech Thee, O my Saviour, to deliver me from all my enemies, visible and invisible, and to bring me, under Thy protection, to the perfection of eternal salvation. **Amen.**

THIRD PRAYER

Our Father - Hail Mary.

O Jesus! Creator of Heaven and earth Whom nothing can encompass or limit, Thou Who dost enfold and hold all under Thy Loving power, remember the very bitter pain.

Thou didst suffer when the Jews nailed Thy Sacred Hands and Feet to the Cross by blow after blow with big blunt nails, and not finding Thee in a pitiable enough state to satisfy their rage, they enlarged Thy Wounds, and added pain to pain, and with indescribable cruelty stretched Thy Body on the Cross, pulled Thee from all sides, thus dislocating Thy Limbs.

I beg of Thee, O Jesus, by the memory of this most Loving suffering of the Cross, to grant me the grace to fear Thee and to Love Thee. **Amen.**

FOURTH PRAYER

Our Father - Hail Mary.

O Jesus! Heavenly Physician, raised aloft on the Cross to heal our wounds with Thine, remember the bruises which Thou didst suffer and the weakness of all Thy Members which were distended to such a degree that never was there pain like unto Thine.

From the crown of Thy Head to the Soles of Thy Feet there was not one spot on Thy Body that was not in torment, and yet, forgetting all Thy sufferings, Thou didst not cease to pray to Thy Heavenly Father for Thy enemies, saying: "Father forgive them for they know not what they do."

Through this great Mercy, and in memory of this suffering, grant that the remembrance of Thy Most Bitter Passion may effect in us a perfect contrition and the remission of all our sins. **Amen**.

FIFTH PRAYER
Our Father – Hail Mary.
O Jesus! Mirror of eternal splendour, remember the sadness which Thou experienced, when contemplating in the light of Thy Divinity the predestination of those who would be saved by the merits of Thy Sacred Passion.

Thou didst see at the same time, the great multitude of reprobates who would be damned for their sins, and Thou didst complain bitterly of those hopeless lost and unfortunate sinners.

Through this abyss of compassion and pity, and especially through the goodness which Thou displayed to the good thief when Thou saidst to him: "This day, thou shalt be with Me in Paradise." I beg of Thee, O Sweet Jesus, that at the hour of my death, Thou wilt show me mercy. **Amen**.

SIXTH PRAYER
Our Father - Hail Mary.
O Jesus! Beloved and most desirable King, remember the grief Thou didst suffer, when naked and like a common criminal.

Thou was fastened and raised on the Cross, when all Thy relatives and friends abandoned Thee, except Thy Beloved Mother, who remained close to Thee during Thy agony and whom Thou didst entrust to Thy faithful disciple when Thou saidst to Mary: "Woman, behold thy son!" and to St. John: "Son, behold thy Mother!"

I beg of Thee O my Saviour, by the sword of sorrow which pierced the soul of Thy holy Mother, to have compassion on me in all my affliction and tribulations, both corporal and spiritual, and to assist me in all my trials, and especially at the hour of my death. **Amen**.

SEVENTH PRAYER

Our Father - Hail Mary.

O Jesus! Inexhaustible Fountain of compassion, Who by a profound gesture of Love, said from the Cross: "I thirst!" suffered from the thirst for the salvation of the human race.

I beg of Thee O my Saviour, to inflame in our hearts the desire to tend toward perfection in all our acts; and to extinguish in us the concupiscence of the flesh and the ardor of worldly desires. **Amen**.

EIGHTH PRAYER

Our Father - Hail Mary.

O Jesus! Sweetness of hearts, delight of the spirit, by the bitterness of the vinegar and gall which Thou didst taste on the Cross for Love of us, grant us the grace to receive worthily.

Thy Precious Body and Blood during our life and at the hour of our death, that they may serve as a remedy and consolation for our souls. **Amen.**

NINTH PRAYER
Our Father – Hail Mary.

O Jesus! Royal virtue, joy of the mind, recall the pain Thou didst endure when, plunged in an ocean of bitterness at the approach of death, insulted, outraged by the Jews.

Thou didst cry out in a loud voice that Thou was abandoned by Thy Father, saying: "My God, My God, why hast Thou forsaken me?"

Through this anguish, I beg of Thee, O my Saviour, not to abandon me in the terrors and pains of my death. **Amen.**

TENTH PRAYER
Our Father – Hail Mary.

O Jesus! Who art the beginning and end of all things, life and virtue, remembers that for our sakes Thou was plunged in an abyss of suffering from the soles of Thy Feet to the crown of Thy Head.

In consideration of the enormity of Thy Wounds, teach me to keep, through pure love, Thy Commandments, whose way is wide and easy for those who love Thee. **Amen.**

ELEVENTH PRAYER

Our Father - Hail Mary.

O Jesus! Deep abyss of mercy, I beg of Thee, in memory of Thy Wounds which penetrated to the very marrow of Thy Bones and to the depth of Thy being, to draw me, a miserable sinner, overwhelmed by my offenses, away from sin and to hide me from Thy Face justly irritated against me, hide me in Thy wounds, until Thy anger and just indignation shall have passed away. **Amen.**

TWELFTH PRAYER

Our Father - Hail Mary.

O Jesus! Mirror of Truth, symbol of unity, bond of charity, remember the multitude of wounds with which Thou wast afflicted from head to foot, torn and reddened by the spilling of Thy adorable Blood. O great and universal pain, which Thou didst suffer in Thy virginal flesh for love of us!

Sweetest Jesus! What is there that Thou couldst have done for us which Thou has not done!

May the fruit of Thy suffering be renewed in my soul by the faithful remembrance of Thy Passion, and may Thy love increase in my heart each day, until I see Thee in eternity: Thou Who art the treasure of every real good and every joy, which I beg Thee to grant me, O Sweetest Jesus, in heaven. **Amen.**

THIRTEENTH PRAYER
Our Father – Hail Mary.

O Jesus! Strong Lion, Immortal and Invincible King, remember the pain which Thou didst endure when all Thy strength, both moral and physical, was entirely exhausted, Thou didst bow Thy Head, saying: "It is consummated!"

Through this anguish and grief, I beg of Thee Lord Jesus, to have mercy on me at the hour of my death when my mind will be greatly troubled and my soul will be in anguish. **Amen.**

FOURTEENTH PRAYER

Our Father – Hail Mary.

O Jesus! Only Son of the Father, Splendour and Figure of His Substance, remember the simple and humble recommendation.

Thou didst make of Thy Soul to Thy Eternal Father, saying: "Father, into Thy Hands I commend My Spirit!" And with Thy Body all torn, and Thy Heart Broken, and the bowels of Thy Mercy open to redeem us, Thou didst Expire.

By this Precious Death, I beg of Thee O King of Saints, comfort me and help me to resist the devil, the flesh and the world, so that being dead to the world I may live for Thee alone.

I beg of Thee at the hour of my death to receive me, a pilgrim and an exile returning to Thee. **Amen.**

FIFTEENTH PRAYER

Our Father – Hail Mary.

O Jesus! True and fruitful Vine! Remember the abundant outpouring of Blood which Thou didst so generously shed from Thy Sacred Body as juice from grapes in a wine press.

From Thy Side, pierced with a lance by a soldier, blood and water issued forth until there was not left in Thy Body a single drop, and finally, like a bundle of myrrh lifted to the top of the Cross Thy delicate Flesh was destroyed, the very Substance of Thy Body withered, and the Marrow of Thy Bones dried up.

Through this bitter Passion and through the outpouring of Thy Precious Blood, I beg of Thee, O Sweet Jesus, to receive my soul when I am in my death agony. **Amen.**

CONCLUSION

O Sweet Jesus! Pierce my heart so that my tears of penitence and love will be my bread day and night; may I be converted entirely to Thee, may my heart be Thy perpetual habitation, may my conversation be pleasing to Thee, and may the end of my life be so praiseworthy that I may merit Heaven and there with Thy saints, praise Thee forever. **Amen.**